To:

_____

I'm gifting this book to you because:

_____

_____

_____

_____

_____

But most of all, because <u>you</u> are
kind of a Big Deal.

From:

_____

PS: Team Gifting Info → BigDeal.ErinKing.com

Praise for
You're Kind of a Big Deal
and Erin King

"We're all facing down challenging scenarios that are out of our control. In *You're Kind of a Big Deal*, Erin King offers a plethora of relatable stories and actionable mindset makeovers so you can better navigate your current season with greater confidence and audacity."

—**Carey Lohrenz,** the US Navy's first female F-14 pilot
and *Wall Street Journal* bestselling author of
Fearless Leadership and *Span of Control*

"Whether you're an entrepreneur or network marketer or you're just looking to ignite more courageous action in your life, *You're Kind of a Big Deal* is the book to help guide you toward living your most extraordinary life."

—**Jessica Herrin,** CEO of Stella & Dot and author of
Find Your Extraordinary

"If you've ever needed a kick in the audacity in the form of a best friend who not only tells you that 'you can do it' but also shows you how, make space on your nightstand for Erin King's *You're Kind of a Big Deal*. With equal parts wisdom and sass, not to mention hilarious storytelling, this book will ignite your intentionality, power up your potential, and level up your life."

—**Laura Gassner Otting,** *Washington Post* bestselling
author of *Limitless*

"Powerful, generous, and *fun*, this book is a gift to any woman who picks it up. Erin spares us the fluff and offers something much more valuable: useful truth and a plan for finding the confidence you are worthy of."

—**Judi Holler**, bestselling author of *Fear Is My Homeboy*

"An honest, funny, strategy-packed ride; I was hooked from the introduction. Erin King brings it with how to have the audacity to go with your gut. Get ready to break glass ceilings, speak your full truth, and start feeling like you can do anything."

—**Andrea Owen**, bestselling author of *Make Some Noise*

"Erin's book is overflowing with so many usable strategies that will help you tap into and turn up your motivation to help you design and create your best life. As always, Erin brings her tough love, wrapped in warm laughter. This is a must-read for every leader—whether you are leading a team of one or one hundred."

—**Petra Kolber**, author of *The Perfection Detox*

"Hilarious, practical, inspiring, and 100 percent authentic! *You're Kind of a Big Deal* is like reading something out of an *SNL* skit but then quickly realizing its message is also deep, impactful, and really frickin' inspiring. Erin King is an absolute master not just at preaching audacity, but at demonstrating it. Her opening story is one of the funniest I've ever heard . . . and the audaciousness continues until the last page. I have never snorted while simultaneously having aha moments more than when reading this book!"

—**Erin Hatzikostas**, author of *You Do You(ish)*

"Erin's voice is a breath of fresh air—like a combo of inspiring coach and close confidant. With candid stories and humor, *You're Kind of a Big Deal* is the perfect guide for women looking to unlock their inner audacity."

—**Erin Falconer**, bestselling author of
How to Get Sh*t Done

"An energetic blend of both compelling stories and practical advice, *You're Kind of a Big Deal* is a powerful page-turner that dares us to elevate our everyday."

—**Vanessa Van Edwards**, bestselling author of *Captivate*

"Filled with entertaining stories, advice, humor, and wisdom, *You're Kind of a Big Deal* is a total game-changer."

—**Heather Monahan**, author of *Overcome Your Villains*
and *Confidence Creator*

"Whether you're a network marketer, an or entrepreneur, or a seasoned leader, or you're brand new to the workforce, this powerful book encourages women to get gutsy and chase down their biggest goals. In fact, the book was so effective, it even gave me (a guy!) the audacity to fully endorse a book written for women. And that's 'kind of a big deal.'"

—**Mark Sanborn**, author of *The Fred Factor*

"Erin King is one of the most authentic and powerful voices in leadership today. In her book *You're Kind of a Big Deal*, she reveals how to step bravely and unapologetically into the life you want and deserve. If you are ready to kick limiting beliefs to the curb and confidently achieve your goals, this book should be at the top of your reading list."

—**Amberly Lago**, expert mindset coach, speaker,
and bestselling author of *True Grit and Grace*

"*You're Kind of a Big Deal* is a fresh peek into one woman's confidence-building journey!"

—**Charlene Walters,** author of *Launch Your Inner Entrepreneur*

"Erin King gets it exactly right. When you dare to activate your audacity, everything changes. If you're ready to clip on your cape, take back your power, and up-level your life, pick up *You're Kind of a Big Deal*!"

—**Jo Miller,** CEO of Be Leaderly and author of *Woman of Influence*

YOU'RE KIND OF A BIG DEAL

YOU'RE
KIND OF A
BIG
DEAL

LEVEL UP
BY UNLOCKING YOUR
AUDACITY

ERIN KING

Mc Graw Hill

NEW YORK CHICAGO SAN FRANCISCO ATHENS LONDON
MADRID MEXICO CITY MILAN NEW DELHI
SINGAPORE SYDNEY TORONTO

1 2 3 4 5 6 7 8 9   LCR   26 25 24 23 22 21

ISBN   978-1-264-26683-8
MHID   1-264-26683-9

e-ISBN   978-1-264-26684-5
e-MHID   1-264-26684-7

Library of Congress Cataloging-in-Publication Data

Names: King, Erin (Erin Gargan), author.
Title: You're kind of a big deal : level up by unlocking your audacity / Erin King.
Description: New York : McGraw Hill, [2021] | Includes bibliographical
   references and index.
Identifiers: LCCN 2021001790 (print) | LCCN 2021001791 (ebook) | ISBN
   9781264266838 (hardback) | ISBN 9781264266845 (ebook)
Subjects: LCSH: Self-realization in women. | Assertiveness in women. | Self-esteem in
   women. | Self-confidence.
Classification: LCC HQ1206 .K466 2021 (print) | LCC HQ1206 (ebook) | DDC
   155.3/3382—dc23
LC record available at https://lccn.loc.gov/2021001790
LC ebook record available at https://lccn.loc.gov/2021001791

McGraw Hill books are available at special quantity discounts to use as premiums and sales promotions or for use in corporate training programs. To contact a representative, please visit the Contact Us pages at www.mhprofessional.com.

This book is for the women in my family who consistently demonstrate that being a Big Deal starts with having a big heart.

For Nana: you were the first person who ever told me to ignore everyone and do it anyway.

For Trudy: how we all miss your warm Currie cackle and straight-shooting tough love.

For my mom, Helen (thank God for Carly Simon); my sisters Shannon and Lauren; my mother-in-law, Charlotte; my aunts Tracy, MB, Kate, Meg, Kathy, and Beth; my cousins Meggie, Maggie, Erin, MAF, Kristine, Alicia, Meg, Leah, Colleen, Nora, Alex, and Kelli.

For my beloved fur baby Stevie Nicks; you sat by my side as I typed every single word of this book. Mommy misses you every minute of every day. I promise to meet you at the Rainbow Bridge my love.

Finally, for my nieces Gracie Maeve and Molly Piper: when the world tries to make you play small, remember that you come from a long line of fiery females who are always here to help you play big.

CONTENTS

CONTENTS

HOW DARE YOU?

The tampons were piled up in the middle of the long conference table. Outside, the deep-blue Pacific Ocean sparkled in the distance beyond the floor-to-ceiling windows. Sitting around the table were not Girl Scouts in a middle school health class, but a dozen tan, buff alpha males. Shifting in their chairs like they had ants in their designer jeans, they looked up; they looked out; they looked down; they looked *anywhere* except directly at the scary sticks of feminine dynamite directly in front of them.

It was 2013 in Newport Beach, California, and I found myself smack-dab in the middle of my very own real-life *Shark Tank* moment. Except there was no Lori. Or Sara. Or even Barbara. Instead, the room was full of dudes who looked like they were straight off their own reality show, one where the opening credits began with a Ferrari screaming into the parking lot of a CrossFit gym, blaring Kanye.

I was looking for this boardroom of fratastic finance bros to back my hot new startup idea. And this idea was hotter than the latest fintech app. Sexier than cryptocurrency. More futuristic than artificial intelligence. What did the world need more than anything? (Dramatic pause.) A tampon delivery service.

As I rattled off my carefully practiced stories (packed full of erotic, enticing nouns like *blood* and *cramps*), I suddenly locked eyes with one particularly tan broski who looked as though he was going to vomit his hundred-dollar sushi lunch all over the beautiful, shiny table.

Instantaneously, I lost all focus and began profusely sweating through my Spanx. My heart began to race, my hands started to shake, and I had to remind myself that this was not one of those dreams where you go to school naked but then wake up. Nope. This was actually happening (not the nudity—although I imagine that at least one of those men wanted to faint assuming I was about to do a product demonstration). Scanning the disgusted, shocked faces of essentially every extra from *The Wolf of Wall Street,* I suddenly found myself sharing in the queasiness of Tan Broski Investor Number Three. My confidence crumbled like the feta on my lunchtime Greek salad (at least I wouldn't be throwing up overpriced sashimi).

I contemplated sprinting straight out of the room. This moment that I had worked so hard to make happen now seemed like an absurd, ridiculous, and just plain *stupid* mistake. Not only did none of the potential investors look interested in my blood-sweat-and-tears venture; they looked like they would rather get a root canal than listen to one more word from Madame Tampon Fairy.

Suddenly, one of the investors, a guy named Todd (there's always a Todd), broke the awkward vibe by grabbing one of my sample tampons and tossing it across the table at another guy. "Dare ya to open one!" he challenged.

"*Ewww*, no way, dude. Dare *you* to!" Todd was pelted in return. Suddenly, to my horror, almost in slow motion, like one of those car accidents that you want to look away from but can't, the world's very first game of tampon-hot-potato broke out. In the middle of an actual boardroom. Right as I made my way through my carefully cultivated pitch deck where I was asking for seven figures of capital. *This never happens on Shark Tank.*

Then I noticed something. Todd's audacious (albeit imma-ture) move had lightened the mood and made the other guys smile and relax for the first time since my train wreck of a pitch. And in that moment of desperation, of nothing-to-lose-ness, I realized something. Todd didn't care if it was unprofessional to throw tampons around a boardroom. Todd wasn't worried the other investors would think he was an idiot. In the absolute best possible way, he straight up *did not care* if it was shocking or offensive to everyone else in the room. So in that moment, I decided to channel my inner Too Tan Todd. I made a split-second decision to say "Screw it" and release my fears of what these guys thought about me and my idea. And in that fleeting moment, just embracing that thought let me lighten up, stop overthink-ing, and let go of the anxiety. I threw out the perfectly rehearsed pitch and the self-judging trash, and I went for it. Like a delusion-ally confident Newport Beach guy hitting on someone way out of his league, I told myself that it was likely they loved it. That it was highly probable I was crushing it. I convinced myself— my sweaty, stammering self—that I had every right to be there, because although they (and the rest of the world) didn't know it yet—I'm kind of a Big Deal. Just like Todd.

Yeah, I know. Thinking like that is insane. Delusional. Cray cray to the max. But you know what else it was? It was *audacious*.

If you've ever wanted to learn what to do *even* when the world says no, *even* when you're going down in flames, *even* when you want to die from embarrassment or cry from frustration or just throw in the dang towel, *please*, please *don't*. You are reading this book for a reason. And that reason is so you can walk away with a few supercharged strategies to help you overcome even the toughest of moments and surprise yourself with what you're truly capable of making happen. Yes, even in the face of the most absurdly massive of barriers. How? By unlocking the inner audacity that is lying dormant inside you at this very moment. And this book is your how-to, go-to guide so you'll know exactly how to channel that audacity into real-life, real-world, real-results action—just like what happened with the Todd Squad in that boardroom turned playground.

Let's flashback to some seriously sweaty Spanx, shall we? Bursting with my newfound BDE (Big Deal Energy—why, what did you think it stood for?), I grabbed the tampon out of Todd's hand and started to use it as my new microphone and my new pointer—and shockingly, the guys started to laugh, lean forward, and pay attention. Miraculously, that tampon transformed into my magic wand as I Harry-Pottered my way through with wizard skills I never knew I possessed. At the end, as if I were floating outside of myself like one of those ghosts at Hogwarts, I watched incredulously as I point-blank asked for the money to launch PMS.com.

The lead investor looked me in the eye and said:

Erin, we obviously don't know much about any of this girl stuff. But what we do know is that good investments come from betting on the jockey, not the horse. You seem like you might make an all-right jockey, so what the heck . . . Did you bring a term sheet?

What I learned from that lucky tampon is that sometimes it takes more than just confidence, preparation, and hard work to win. Sometimes it takes not just daring boldly, but daring boldly even if it might shock or offend—like a presentation with a tampon microphone. Sometimes going way beyond confident to borderline crazy is the only way to flip the win switch in the highest-stakes scenarios. Sometimes it's something as silly as rerouting a grown-man game of tampon-hot-potato that opens life-changing opportunities. Sometimes it takes *knowing* that you are kind of a Big Deal, even if an entire room of very intimidating individuals might disagree. Sometimes triumphing over adversity and busting through barriers are not outcomes that come in perfectly confident, prepared, and polished packages delivered right to our door. Instead, they come in slightly more audacious ones.

Whatever you're up against in your life that feels too big, too scary, too intimidating, too "Hell no, that's not possible!," please hear me on this: if I can raise seven figures from the totally grossed-out Real Bachelors of Orange County using a tampon microphone, you can too. You can *do the thing*. You can ask for the thing. You can quit the thing. You can start the thing. You can be the thing. You can make even your most secret, massive, moonshot dreams come true. You can demand that your deepest desires become your most rad of realities.

So let's just say what you're facing down in this season isn't a *Shark Tank* nightmare—fair enough and good call. But I know that you know you've had at least (at least!) one time where you were starting something so awesome, so fantastic, and you were so pumped, so excited, so ready to rock—until someone else's judgment or disapproval, shock, negativity, confusion, dislike, or *straight-up revulsion* made you trip, crash, and burn. Where someone's "No, girl" instead of "Go, girl!" evaporated every ounce of excitement and made you question not just your plan but yourself.

Maybe it wasn't a team of investors, but maybe it was your friend, your boss, your client, your colleague—even a family member—who responded in a way you weren't expecting. And because you weren't prepared for how to handle a big, messy, unfavorable reaction, the pail of cold water quickly extinguished your feisty flames. And maybe that was what nudged you back into your cozy comfort zone, where you're sitting now, reading this book.

And so maybe instead of doing that thing, you put it off for another day. Tomorrow. Next week. Next year. Next time. Maybe you put off becoming a mom. Or a dog mom. Or a speaker. Or an author. Or an artist, photographer, or yoga instructor. Maybe you put off starting your own business or launching that new venture. Or asking for that raise, promotion, or new job. Or becoming a sales leader. Maybe you put off finally facing your debt problem or your addiction. Maybe you put off that new healthier lifestyle program. Maybe you put off buying a house or starting that home project. Or going to college. Or going back to college. Or getting the certification. Or running the marathon. Or learning the language. Or paying off the loan. Or moving. Or traveling. Or getting your head, your heart, your soul, or all three back on track after heartbreak. *Or all these things!*

How insane is it that it takes only one scary situation, one snarky comment, one silent disapproval, one over-the-top reaction, and *boom!*—you're no longer in the game.

Despite your emotions, despite any barriers, and no matter what everyday crap or life-altering challenges you are dealing with in this moment, let me say that *you*, my friend, are kind of a Big Deal. Yes, you. Yes, right now. A Big [*insert your preferred profanity here*] Deal. And knowing, believing, and *loving* your Big Deal self with upper-level audacity is the only true obstacle between your current situation and the elevated, extraordinary one you're made for.

See, what's probably actually holding you back—from what you secretly wish you could do, from making that progress, from sustaining your momentum, or maybe even from just getting started in the first place—is simple. And it can be overcome. Reversed. Conquered. Rearview-mirrored. And you and I are going to do it together. One audacious action at a time.

OK, let's take a quick timeout before we dive in: you might be thinking, *Whoa, wait a second. Isn't being audacious a bad thing?* Touché, fair question, and it depends on whom you're asking. Brace yourself for this one: A 2018 study conducted by Pew Research asked 4,573 Americans to share words that they thought best described traits that society does and doesn't value for each gender. Wait for it . . . the top three positive traits for women were *beautiful*, *kind*, and *compassionate*. And the top three for men were *leader*, *ambitious*, and *strong*. Wait, there's more: on top of this most devastating data, those exact same "male" adjectives, when used to describe women, instead of being similarly positive, were ranked as "negative" or "neutral." Yes, even in today's #TimesUp and #GoGirl world. You probably wish you could unread that.

Have you ever heard of even one negotiation, one business deal, or one war that was successful using solely beauty, kindness, or compassion? Even Cleopatra's legendary beauty didn't drive her success in ancient Egypt. A few years ago, coins with Cleopatra's "average-looking" (guess the gender of the reporter who wrote that) face on them were discovered, and the world had a meltdown. Wait, what? Cleopatra was powerful because she was smart, strategic, and cunning, not because she was a smoky-eyeliner hottie who slept her way to victory. The head of the Sphinx might as well have been replaced with the mind-blown emoji.

Even Mr. Dictionary himself, Noah Webster, seems a little foggy on exactly what it means to be audacious. In his semi-two-faced definition, he says that audacity is both "a willingness to take risks" and "rude or disrespectful behavior." Webster, *what?* So does being audacious make you a total legend or a total jerk? Well, it's really in the eye of the beholder, isn't it?

Was Rosa Parks a disrespectful seamstress or a brave hero? Was Marie Curie an absentee mother or a bold scientist? Was Florence Nightingale a disobedient daughter or a pioneering nurse?

Was Amelia Earhart a reckless woman or a daring pilot? Is Malala Yousafzai an impertinent young woman or a fearless warrior?

What is the common denominator you see in each of these dynamos? They absorbed the refusal, threats, disapproval, and mockery of their respective worlds and used that negative feedback as courageous caffeine to energize their respective missions. And how you migrate your dreams from private thoughts to public realities is no different. Sure, maybe your enemy is the rank-and-file leadership team at your company, or an important relationship in your life you're afraid to jeopardize, or the homogenous familial, societal, religious, or academic culture in which you've been pleasantly partaking for most of your life. But when it comes to reinventing, reprogramming, or restarting, you must answer one question for yourself: Are you willing to live boldly even if it might shock (or offend) others? *Living boldly* sounds great, but *shocking and offending others*? The reason most people still are stuck, mediocre, whiny, unfulfilled, and hopeless is because their answer to that question is a safe, cozy, resounding *Ummm*, "Thanks but no thanks."

See, you may *think* the reason you aren't more audacious already or haven't done the thing already is because you fear a specific someone's judgment or rejection of your choices, your actions, or your initiatives, but that's not actually what's going on. Too often, what you really fear, what we all really fear, is that people aren't rejecting our *thing* or *idea* or *ask*, but instead they're rejecting *us. We're terrified of their rejection of us as a human being.* So when you think about your deepest, darkest journaled secrets, when you think about what comes to mind when you gaze out over a cityscape or an ocean, when you watch a movie or hear a song that leaves you with the most unruly and untamed of desires, whose reaction is holding you back from transforming those thoughts into things? Do you truly desire your future reality more than you fear your family, friends, neighbors, coworkers, or maybe even *your own* reactions in the present moment? If you are nodding your head yes, audacity is your answer.

After all, people can still love *you* without loving your *thing*. And if they don't, well, are you sure they're really your people?

When you think of people you truly admire, living or dead, know personally or not, how would you articulate what it is you applaud them for? It's likely that on levels obvious or not so obvious, they're better at "politely" ignoring anyone who is offended by their refusal to play smaller. It's likely that they're better at not internalizing someone else's shock or disapproval at their personal or professional life choices. It's likely that they know, without a shadow of doubt, that they are kind of a Big Deal, and they don't let *anyone* tell them otherwise. They make their stance clear, not in a braggy, narcissistic, or annoying way, but in a BDE kind of way.

What's a BDE kind of way? Well, first, let's start with what it's *not*. BDE is not about listening to one of the most ridiculous pieces of advice people love to give: "You shouldn't care what anyone thinks about you!" *Yeah*. *Right*. People who say they "don't care what *anyone* thinks about them" are full of a certain stinky emoji. Because people who actually don't care what anyone thinks about them are usually a-holes or psychopaths. It's only natural to want the people we love to also love our choices. Approval, whether in the form of a *verbal atta girl* or a digital Instagram *like*, floods our brains with dopamine and makes us feel *good*. But the truth is, and we all know this to be true, intuition is individual. Only *you* can know what's right for *you*. Your strongest internal guide does not exist within others for a reason. So when you're at a crossroads and the stakes are at their highest, it's not that you don't care what anyone thinks, but instead you care *more* what *you* think about your choices. Tuning into that decision, trusting your instinct, and operating audaciously is exactly how you unlock your BDE.

For example, let's hop back to those people who came to mind for you a few moments ago. It's highly likely their BDE was their "secret superpower" they used to actually accomplish the lofty goals they set for themselves. Their BDE is the understated self-swagger they've relied on to design a life they love, despite the protests, judgments, and confusion of even their most favorite people. And here's the best news: you, right now, have *identical* potential. You already possess the exact same BDE. It's just waiting for activation like a daring, intuitive debit card. And over the next nine chapters, you'll internalize how a few of the most audacious women I know leverage their BDE. You'll understand how you can trigger micro-moment magic so you can level up how you approach your everyday with totally transformative results. And you'll turn on the triumphs you know are 1,000 percent possible for you personally and professionally like never before.

Now, as I mentioned earlier, using BDE to activate your audacity is not even remotely close to an excuse to run through life like a self-centered jerk doing whatever you want all the time with no regard for anyone's feelings. Nooooo! No, no, nope. Those folks are the kind of humans you likely found very easy to socially distance yourself from during the pandemic, and for good reason. It's likely that you share my belief that the only secret to a life well lived is one that is deeply rooted in love, kindness, and serving our fellow humans with empathy and compassion. My recommendation is not to embrace your audacity as some binary, constant, all-or-nothing concept. I think about it more like a volume knob that you can dial up or dial down as you see fit—not as the world, your family, your partner, your boss, your kids, or your neighbors see fit—but as *you* see fit. And each situation calls for a different decibel.

Like a cocktail party where the music starts out low and sophisticated, but then by the end of the night has become, let's say, a bit louder and less sophisticated, activating your audacity is about, one, recognizing those high-stakes, critical situations where your volume is too low and, two, doing something about it. Maybe it started off too low; maybe you turned it down; or maybe someone else turned it down for you. However it got there, this book is about preparing, evaluating, and daring to make the decision to turn up your volume, your truth, your bravery, your conviction, your drive, or whatever it is you need in that moment. Yes, even if it's scary. Yes, even if (when) people don't like it. But this is your life. This is your party. And when it's your party, it's your playlist.

Why am I so passionate about helping you crank up the volume of your level of gutsy? Because after starting three companies and speaking with thousands of women at conferences around the world, both in person and online, I've heard the same heart-wrenching stories over and over about what gets us stuck. What makes us sigh. What deflates our brilliance balloons. What makes us play small. What makes us shelf our success. What makes us quit. What bums us the heck out. What shuts us up. What holds us back. What stops us from asking for it. What stops us from taking it, doing it, being it, and breathing it. And through my personal and professional experiences experimenting with all the volume levels, all the playlists, and all the pushback, I've learned *a lot* about what definitely does *not* help a gal level up in this wild world. I've also, thankfully, learned a little bit about what does. And those little bits of "Well, that worked!" are what I offer for your consideration. If you're interested in how you can finally step (and maybe even stomp) into your most audacious Big Deal self, you're going to absolutely rip through the next nine chapters. Together, we'll travel through stories, strategies, and tactics from my experiences and those of my friends, clients, and mentors. I've curated the best bits that radically transformed both my and their lives for the most beautiful better, with the highest of hopes that you'll be audacious enough to do the same.

So let's break down our game plan with some details. We'll begin by exploring some deeply entrenched behaviors that you might not even know are some of the real reasons you can't get "there." By the end of this book, you'll be equipped with strategies and tactics to unlearn:

- Worrying about what others think about you and your choices

- Feeling guilty about not being what people need you to be for them

- Comparing yourself to everyone else online (and in real life)

- Feeling "behind" where you think you should be at this point

- Stressing about being underprepared or underqualified

- Fearing mediocrity and/or failure

- Sabotaging your own efforts

- Seeking unhealthy approval from friends and family, coworkers and bosses, or even perfect strangers on the internet

- Devaluing yourself—your time, your heart, your mind, your soul

Once we've unpacked all of those (don't you feel more audacious already just reading that list?), we'll migrate into exactly how you can start (or restart or sustain):

- Overcoming the obstacles standing between you and your biggest goals

- Performing at your best level professionally and personally

- Loving your current life while moving with intention toward your future

- Experiencing more happiness and delight in your relationships

- Taking on the world with more energy and determination.

- Knowing that your place in life has a clear purpose

- Navigating challenging situations at work more effectively

- Feeling more relaxed in social settings with new people

- Thinking healthier and more positive thoughts on a daily basis

At the end of each chapter, we're not just going to nod our heads passively. No, no, friend. We're going to "seal in" our mental practice by rolling up our sleeves and doing the work. We're not here to just read about it; we're here to take action so we can *be* about it, which is why there's a Big Deal Diary section at the end of each chapter to help you chart your most audacious actions. Even if it might be tempting to skip those sections (kind of like when you drop your knees for a second during plank in an exercise class), please don't. The only person you are cheating there is yourself, so try and commit to being brave enough to seek those tough answers. Translating words off the pages into actual wins in your life doesn't happen by skipping reps.

Whether you decide to use a Big Deal Diary to write down your answers (which you can find at bigdeal.erinking.com) or your own notebook, planner, or even Post-it® notes, is totally up to you. Writing down your thoughts and feelings after each chapter will cover the emotional and psychological gamut. It's also the most direct route to help you tackle, unpack, and review or restart whatever season you find yourself in at this moment.

Sometimes you'll walk away from a Big Deal Diary session finding that you've ignited unstoppable momentum toward a new, bolder mindset with clear action steps for an audacious decision. Other times you'll discover new revelations you perhaps didn't truly know about yourself. Occasionally you might laugh. Frequently you'll likely cry as you shed those layers with the catharsis of a good chemical peel for the soul. You'll likely feel mortified and empowered and everything in between. It's extreme journaling. And it's not for the faint of heart, but it is for the audacious of spirit. And don't worry. None of our exercises will involve explaining tampon absorbencies to a group of Brody Jenners who'd rather be playing Golden Tee and drinking craft beer.

So, you Big Deal brilliant babe, are you ready to do this with me?

If so, get ready for our first soul skinny dip in Audacity Lake. Even though it sounds nuts, please humor me for a second and say out loud, "I'm kind of a Big Deal." I encourage you to say it loudly, even shout it, but if you're not there yet, I'll let it slide if you can only whisper it quietly. (We'll get there.) I'll wait. Oh, you're smiling? Rolling your eyes? Changing your mind? You think this woo-woo hippie-dippie crap doesn't work? Listen to me. (Is this thing on? *Taps tampon.*) I know we've only just met, but if you can trust me, I can assure you, you will not regret this ride.

OK now, like you *really* mean it: *I'm kind of a Big Deal.*

Sorry, you're what? (One last time but with passion!)

I'M KIND OF A BIG DEAL!

Yes, you are. How are you feeling right now? Like a weirdo but an empowered, excited one? Perfect.

Now, turn the page, friend, and let's begin our audacious adventure.

CHAPTER 1

TELL YOU WHAT YOU WANT, WHATCHA REALLY REALLY WANT

The tears plopped into the foamy top of my Guinness. If you've ever been that 22-year-old crying in a bar, you know no one likes that girl. Not even that girl likes that girl. The whole place just wants to boot her sad, beer-tear self outta there so everyone can go back to playing flip cup in peace. But I'm getting ahead of myself. Let's rewind all the way back to 1½ pints ago.

I was ponied up at an Irish pub in Baltimore whining to my poor roomie about my boss, my dating life, my finances, my fami-

1

ly—I was basically face-blast bitching at this poor gal to the point that she finally cut me off: "Erin! OMG. *Stop*. I get it: 'Everything is wrong; something is missing; everything is disappointing'; blah blah blah. So what exactly is it that you *do* want?" Speechless (finally), I realized I had absolutely no idea how to answer her fairly simple question, other than, "*Not this!*"

You may have picked up this book because you are feeling a little like beer-tear 22-year-old me. Maybe you're out of sorts; in a rut; feeling stuck, sad, annoyed, lost, or even a dash of all of the above. Or maybe you're crystal clear on what it is you're chasing down, what it is you need to rise above, and what it is you need to *feel*, and you're just looking for the *how*. If you are the latter, congrats on knowing your *why*. You may pass Go, collect $200, and proceed to Chapter 2. See you there in a few.

But if you aren't exactly sure what's wrong or what's in your way—you just know something *is*—let's unpack it together, right now. Wherever you are reading this—on a plane, on a train, or in your favorite Lux Lyft—do me a favor. I'm going to ask you to please close this book, shut your eyes, and take three big deep breaths in through your nose and let them out through your mouth. Let's do it together right now. (Yes, I'm asking you to take a pause on reading this book when we're only on Chapter 1.)

Welcome back. Don't you feel the tiniest bit better already? Same! OK, enough Zen stuff: let's roll up our sleeves and unpack this thing properly.

While only you can define what your leveled-up life might look and feel like, I'm going to make a fairly safe assumption and say that no matter what the specifics are, you're likely in the mood or mindset to discover new ways to live a life that you really, truly, madly love. Like a life you love so much that if your life were a person, you would want to marry it. Sounds like a deceptively simple goal, but if it were, we wouldn't be reading books, listening to podcasts, sharing motivational quotes, doing health challenges, journaling, planning, affirming, and downward-dogging our asses off, now would we?

See, the thing about the goal of living a life you love is it's a moving-target goal. It's not like weighing 140 pounds, making a million dollars in one year, or cutting down your social media time to less than an hour a day (#mygoals). It's not a goal with a clear end point, where once you hit it, you think, *yay! I did it!* No. Living a life that you love is bigger. It's messier. It's more complicated. And it changes. *A lot.* It's not a mountain you just climb to the top of and then sit on for the rest of your life. Because staring at the view from the top is spectacular, until you get bored, tired, or hungry or your gaze falls on an even *more* spectacular peak to summit.

What made you happy last year or five years ago might not be making you as thrilled today. Or maybe you thought someone, someplace, or something new would be the ticket, only to discover it was quite the opposite. Maybe you're currently smack-dab in a situation that you know is right for you, but you're finding that you have to fight Mr.-Miyagi-and-Daniel-san style to defend it, nurture it, or save it. Maybe you can't define what it is yet, but you have that restless, itching vibe that's letting you know that it's long overdue that you figure it out. No matter what season you are weathering right now, what we all know to be true is that you cannot possibly achieve—for now at least—what you haven't precisely identified. So together, we're going to stop wallowing, wishing, and bitching. We're going to step away from the fog machine (is that still a thing?) toward the light and define with crystal clarity exactly what it is you need to unlock your biggest, most bodacious potential. Doesn't that sound fantastic? I know. But before we get started, there is one thing we need to go ahead and address.

THE BIG MISTAKE

If GIFs could exist inside books, this is where I would put one of Julia Roberts in *Pretty Woman* holding up her Beverly Hills shopping bags and saying, "Big mistake. Big. *Huge*." Because it's the biggest mistake that we all don't even realize we're making. It's a misstep akin to building the foundation for your success headquarters right smack-dab on an earthquake fault line.

When you feel trapped, restless, or unfulfilled, when you want to shake up your current reality or level up to the next chapter of your life, where do you typically start? If you're like most people, your knee-jerk reaction is probably to start to look around. Maybe you start by looking for answers from the people you trust, like your friends, your family, your romantic partner, or that really enlightened Starbucks barista. You might look externally to those neighbors or coworkers who seem to "have their shit together" to help solve the puzzle of where to best spend your precious time and energy. And when you really run out of patience during your search, you might ask them, "Well, what do *you* think I should do?" And when *their* answers still don't cut it, you might turn to the most credible and sage of sources: the internet. Suddenly it's 3 a.m., and you watch as your fingers are typing the most absurd questions into that blank little bar with the same high hopes you had for that magic 8 ball during your sixth grade sleepover. Ah, yes, surely the Google genie will grant the answers to your most mystifying life questions.

Here's the thing: you can ask every cousin and Nordstrom's salesperson under the sun, and you can Google until your fingers fall off, but you know, deep down, that you are wasting your most precious, non-reclaimable resource. There is truly only *one* way to sort out the sadness over your stuckness, and that is to crank up the volume on your inner GPS lady. What would actually happen if you listened to that turn-by-turn guidance, that "higher you" that secretly was already programmed to know the right route for your life's journey? See, here's the thing: discovering your path to positivity, happiness, and success actually has nothing to do with searching and everything to do with authorizing. (And I don't mean credit cards.) No, locating your lane begins when you have the audacity to authorize your heart to tell you what, deep down, you surreptitiously already know. Your intuition, your internal GPS, is fully charged and standing by, locked and loaded to deliver that glorious guidance for exactly what it is your soul seeks.

When you authorize yourself to be gutsy enough to listen, you'll discover those precious answers that the world's largest search engine will never come even remotely close to delivering. When you authorize yourself to stop looking around and start listening within, you'll finally know with crystal clarity the right road for you. And if you'll just join me for a quick flashback to a particularly pathetic buzzed boo-hoo, I'll prove it to you.

Discovering your path to positivity, happiness, and success actually has nothing to do with searching and everything to do with authorizing.

FROM WHINING TO SHINING

Baltimore, Maryland (known to the locals as *Smalltimore* because everyone is one connection away from knowing everyone else), is a lovely place where most locals proudly follow a delightful, predetermined "standard life plan." The typical life recipe in MD is one part crab cakes, one part football, and two parts family tradition.

Broken down, the Baltimore/Smalltimore milestone checklist goes something like this: You live in the city and get drunk in dark, historical bars until you're 25 (where the beer tears transpired). You get married by 30 at the latest and pop out 2.1 to 3.5 kids. You finance a nice big house out in the burbs and furnish it to Pinterest perfection with the holy trifecta of Pottery Barn, West Elm, and HomeGoods. You "Live, Laugh, Love" while working your nine-to-five job. You drive in 2 hours of apocalyptic traffic to visit Ocean City, Maryland in the summer and hang out with your friends from high school and ultimately experience a fun, safe, enjoyable life until you die. Then your friends and family throw you a banger of a funeral party because (1) a lot of people on the East Coast are Irish and their wakes are more fun than most people's weddings, and (2) even if you aren't Irish, people from Smalltimore (and most small towns, really) know how to party better than anyone. When all is said and done, you look down from heaven with a satisfied smile, fist-bumping your parents who, while you were all on earth, lived within driving distance of you and your gorgeous, perfect children. Life? Check. And cheers!

Now, if you're nodding your head like, "*Yes*! Sounds perfect!" #1 YAY—do it! And #2—trust me; I was more than happy with my standard life plan subscription until one fateful business trip to sunny Southern California.

I will never forget almost driving that PT Cruiser rental off the side of the Pacific Coast Highway when, as I came around a curving hill, the gleaming, azure Pacific Ocean suddenly opened up in front of me with breathtaking beauty. I had never seen anything like that in my entire life. Like a total psycho, without even thinking I (or I guess my "higher me") said, out loud, to no one, "Someday, I will live here." I remember it coming out of my mouth and literally surprising me. Like I spoke without meaning to. It was like my internal posh-voiced GPS was politely but firmly informing me, "Dahling, sorry to interrupt, but . . . you've arrived!" Have you ever had that feeling of being so drawn to a place that it's like you've somehow been there before? If you have, you know it's almost like when you first fall in love with a person—butterflies and back sweat included!

Fast-forward a bit to when I landed back in Smalltimore; I just couldn't get what I had seen and experienced out of my mind. I just kept turning down the volume on that velvet British voice urging me to get off the "highway" (the East Coast term for big road) and onto the "freeway" (the West Coast term for big road). For over two years, I muted this pull toward the Pacific Ocean because a West Coast detour simply wasn't listed anywhere on my standard-issue life plan checklist. Instead, like most of us do when we're too wimpy to try something scary, I complained about it. Constantly. To anyone who would listen.

Which brings us back to my boo-hoo barstool moment where my friend said "Erin, *shut up* about California already! Everyone knows you'll never actually go. You'll be right here in 30 years, just like the rest of us. Let it go!"

Like Marty McFly who goes nuts when someone calls him chicken, that snarky comment was the match my dried-tinder mind needed. Instead of letting go, pulling on my conformity cardigan, and muting my GPS for eternity, something shifted. My tears evaporated, and the navigation volume was cranked to a level that could only be stopped by making the damn turn! Later that night, I watched in shaky disbelief as my fingers jerked the wheel, made a hard left, and booked that one-way ticket to LAX. But it wasn't booking the ticket that terrified me. Like most times when you're making big moves, it was the thought of having to *tell* everyone I'd booked it that had me sweating in my Steve Maddens. Because the truth is that oftentimes it's not our fear of taking the actual action that holds us back; it's the fear of everyone else's *reaction* to it. And if you hail from a certain crew or clan of people, this fear exists for good reason.

> It's not our fear of taking the actual action that holds us back; it's the fear of everyone else's <u>reaction</u> to it.
>
> #BIGDEALBOOK

When I broke the news, my tight-knit family and lifelong friends were more than underwhelmed: they were shocked, outraged, confused, and really hurt. My typically sweet and loving dad was so beside himself that he threatened to cut me out of his will if I left! What? A move to a beach town is a matter of life and death now? My friends I'd known for years were understandably offended. *What was wrong with Baltimore? Weren't they good enough for me and my fancy-pants California dreams?*

If you've ever made a highly unpopular deletion decision: to move, to quit, to decline, to opt out, you know that the bigger your action or change, the bigger other people's reactions. And those big unfavorable reactions from the ones we love make us feel like we're stepping in cement when we're trying to travel through the front door of our dreams. It's sticky, it's messy, it's scary, and if you stop too long to wallow around in it, it will trap you until the end of time. And even though we know that others' reactions to us are just reflections of themselves, even though we know that people are viewing our choices through their life lens and how it makes *them* feel, it still doesn't make it any easier.

Unfavorable reactions from the ones we love can feel like stepping in cement when we're trying to travel through the front door of our dreams.

#BIGDEALBOOK

While I still detest upsetting or disappointing anyone, as cliché as it sounds, moving across the country with my clothes in garbage bags (what 25-year-old actually owns proper luggage?) sparked a rebirth in my soul that I didn't consciously know I even needed. But my inner GPS lady sure as hell did. And so does yours. See, the thing with your gut guide is while she comes with mighty, magical judgment, she is missing one functionality: a mute button. And so the only way you can ever actually silence your inner GPS British lady is to follow the directions she demands of you. When your heart is on fire for something or your "higher you" just *knows* something you don't, it's pretty much a complete waste of your time and energy to try and dump cold water on it. In the end, it just doesn't work. And that really sucks, because daring to live a great adventure and boldly chase down an extraordinary life usually comes with a hefty price tag. The cost is that oftentimes the people you love most might be shocked. They might feel hurt. Worst of all, they might even be offended, like my Baltimore friends and family initially were. The question to ask yourself is: Is that a price you are willing to pay? It's such a critical query because if the answer is no, then why not free yourself? Release your restlessness and snuggle back into your version of Smalltimore—whether it's a place, a job, a crew, a habit, or whatever you are fighting to get good with. Because you don't need a GPS if you choose to stay in a place where you already know all the back roads by heart. And to be sure, there's an exceptional beauty in choosing that route. Savor that satisfaction and release the rest!

You may have already had firsthand experience with the ugly truth about listening to your inner GPS. The catch that comes with leveling up your life is that it's difficult to risk hurting the ones you love as you chase down your dreams. But for some of us, the only way we'll ever discover who we really are, outside of the expectations of a certain work situation, culture, family, or life, is by going out on our own. Sometimes you just have to crawl out on the limb toward the end of the skinny branch with no safety net, no support system, and no "standard life plan" checklist—and sometimes, it's only there that you'll find the space, the fear, and the freedom to actually meet yourself, maybe for the first time. And the nonsexy fine print is that once you do, it's highly likely that you'll never look back. Or if you do, it's probably not going to look the same. And it's that harsh finality of "you can't go back"–ness that keeps us stuck and cozy and attempting to mute those new directions over and over again.

So here's what I invite you to process for a bit. The truth is, if you *want something so badly* that it won't leave you alone no matter how many months or years you give it to settle down, work itself out, or get out of your system, more often than not, it's not going to go away. It's just not. It's also likely that should you decide to finally listen to your inner GPS lady there *is no way* to make that turn without ruffling at least a few feathers.

Please hear me on this: If you aren't changing, you really are choosing. You are choosing to stay where you are. You are choosing to be with whom you're with. You're choosing to invest where you're investing. Warning: more warnings ahead—deciding to *stop* the thing or *start* the thing, or to *leave* the person or *join* the person, is, in a way, a lose-lose decision. Why? Because when you take a big action, make a big change, or make a big move, someone, somewhere, even if you are a *saint*, is not going to like it. In fact, if we're being real, people might even hate it. But the lose-lose is that at the same time this is happening, you are the only one who can tell yourself what you want, even if you feel like a total B while doing it. You are the only one who can pull the trigger and book the ticket or start the venture or yank the rip-cord. You're the one who has to listen to the annoying GPS lady on repeat in your soul for the rest of your life. Not them—*you*. And if you're waiting for her to just stop on her own, waiting for the magical moment when everyone loves your big choice? You'll be waiting for an eternity. And despite our best anti-aging efforts, I hate to tell ya, but we don't have that long.

Now maybe you don't need or want to move 3,000 miles away from where you live. Maybe your dream doesn't require you to give away half of your H&M go-tos so you can fit all your worldly belongings in garbage bags to fly cross-country to La-La Land. Maybe you don't want to travel at all, especially in a post-COVID world. But where else, *how* else, can you create the *space* you need in your life to make sure you can even hear your inner GPS lady? Is it getting up earlier for some power-fully productive time in the morning? Is it trading your Netflix time for a device-free walk around the block? Is it taking a more intentional shower where you refuse to think about your to-do list, but you take those 5 to 10 minutes to just listen? Is it just taking that first step (as you did when you started reading this book) toward contemplating a new deal or a new story for your life? Maybe it's admitting to yourself that there's an area of your life you've been avoiding or ignoring because when you really give it a good hard look, what you see makes you extremely *uncomfortable*?

Selecting everyone else's happiness, preferences, or goals over your own is the path of least resistance. Sure, it makes for fric-tionless relationships. You'll definitely win a popularity contest of your family, neighborhood, team, book club, or friend group, but if you've been feeling that "itch" or that "ughhh" or that "time to shake things up" pull on your heart, you simply *can-not* prioritize everyone else's draft of your life story. Because you will, without a shadow of doubt, lose the "love-your-life" con-test with yourself. And should you choose that, you will find that you've expedited your life to that awful day you see only in bad movies where the main character is looking in the mirror with horror because she doesn't recognize the person staring back at her. (And I'm not talking about a simple surface something a few shots of vitamin B, aka Botox, can fix.) Doing what you "should" do simply to avoid making someone else unhappy is a devastat-ing way to go through life. More than that, as my friend Shelley Brown says, it's total "BullShould." The simple act of choosing "should" over "good" is your fastest route to travel from *anything is possible* straight over to *I'll just be over here giving up*! The should life, for the most part, is certainly not the good life. So why do so many people that you and I both know keep "shoulding" all over themselves?

IT TAKES GUTS TO GO WITH YOUR GUT

It takes guts to go with your gut. And I'm not talking about pizza cravings in a Poundemic. No doubt, it's super-crazy hard to go in a different direction than the one that you thought you would, or think you should, or even tougher, the one everyone around you expects you would. It's monumentally challenging to acknowledge your intuition and go with your gut, but *it is not impossible.*

Case in point: I'll never forget hearing my dear friend from college, Cara O'Connor, tell me, her voice shaking, "She's been in a terrible accident. She's in a coma, and we're not sure she's going to make it." Cara lives in the same house her family lived in a century ago and her early twenties-aged sister, Carly, had been in a terrible car accident the night before that left her unconscious and fighting for her life. The doctors said she might not ever recover. Might never walk. Might never talk. They prepared the O'Connors to expect the worst.

Can you imagine someone saying that about a member of your family? Over the next two years, Cara watched day by excruciating day as a team of nurses rehabilitated her sister and helped her relearn how to do every single basic human function. And when she eventually did start walking and even talking, Cara's inner GPS lady began screaming at her unrelentingly and she couldn't shut her up.

Let's back up, for a second, to before Carly's tragic accident. You know that friend who, when you were in your twenties, was essentially the It Girl of your crew? Yep. That was and is Cara. Just like the infamous Andie Anderson of *How to Lose a Guy in Ten Days*, Cara was and is a strong woman with a killer girl crew, rocking her dream job, and working for a global beauty company's corporate office in downtown New York. Cara was climbing the creative ladder, on track to be one of the company's key executives, living in a spacious place downtown (which is a rarity in NYC), partying on the weekends, and living her best gal-from-out-of-a-rom-com life.

And have you ever had something so traumatic happen to you where you find yourself suddenly feeling like none of what mattered before *that thing* matters anymore? That's exactly where she was: restless, stuck, and processing the fact that those countless hours testing of various waterproof mascaras didn't hold the critical impact in the world she once thought it did. So she started journaling, as we do, and one morning she wrote: "I want to help heal people. I want to save other Carlys in the world."

By authorizing her internal GPS lady to speak on paper, the hard left turn on her wheel of life was initiated. Cara began googling (note the order of operations there: soul-search and listen first; Google-search and act second), and phrases like "Certification to help brain trauma patients" and "where to learn to rehabilitate seriously injured patients" began appearing in her search bar. A few weeks later, she had a plan. She was going back to school. She was going to get a degree. She was going to give up her glamorous present in pursuit of not just a new career, but a full-on new life mission.

You might be thinking, *Wow, people must have been blown away by her kind, brave pivot. They must have been sooooo supportive of her valiant, selfless reinvention.* And, um, yes, kind of, sort of, they were. (Voice goes up here. Always beware of the voice getting higher when listening for untruths.) The truth is, many people cheered her on to her face, as that was the only socially acceptable response; but to be honest, I caught wind of more than one "Has she completely lost her mind?" commentary. (From our Irish friends the response verbatim was, "Sure, she's gone mad as a hatter.")

And I'm regretful to admit I was one of them! I'd be lying if deep down that wasn't my initial reaction. And as her crew who loved her and wanted what was "best" for her, we had a *lot* of questions. Was she sure she wanted to walk away from her fat paycheck? From a super-hip company? Playing with all the most fabulous, expensive makeup and skin care products and magnetic eyelashes? Was she sure she wanted to freeze a decade-long trajectory to blow it all up and start over? And even then, would she ever make nearly as much money? Or have an iota of the same amount of fun and creative freedom? And most selfishly, how would *we* be able to afford our anti-aging product army without her hookups? (Remember, reactions are just reflections. How people react to you is almost always a reflection of them and how your actions make *them* feel.)

I remember looking at her steadfast spirit with awe, asking her how she was able to tune everyone out and stay so sure of such a wild move, of such an uncertain future! Without even a *pause* in her signature bubbly voice (you know, like that moment in *Legally Blonde* where Elle Woods says "Happy people just don't kill their husbands"), Cara said with complete conviction: "Erin. Duh. You can never lose when you go with your gut. You just can't."

Like Elle Woods winning that trial and like Cara reinventing her life, that advice is the most deceptively simple advice in the history of sage suggestions! You and I both know that the harsh reality is this: going with your gut truly does take *guts*. Let's skim over just a few of the nonsexy logistics that were necessary to actualize Cara's new adventure. To make this positively outrageous professional pivot, Cara sold most of her stuff. She canceled all her memberships and subscriptions. She moved from buzzing, glam New York to attend the program she got into and could afford, which happened to be located in a decidedly less "sophisticated" Midwest state. (Pleading the Fifth here.) At 34, while many of our old college pals were mortgaging houses and making babies, she found herself sharing an apartment with a crew of twenty-something roommates. *Roommates.* But Cara was a woman on a mission. She washed her face (with drugstore face wash), cracked open the books, and got down to the business of transforming her skill set to include those of a professional, certified healer. She was basically off the grid for nearly three years—studying, working, and even (gasp!) doing her own hair and nails.

Fast-forward to today, and Dr. Cara O'Connor, has published an esteemed academic research paper on occupational therapy treatments. Now instead of ranking bronzers, she spends her days helping people just like her sister, Carly, walk and talk again after traumatic brain injuries. She is making less money for more hours. And she is *way way way* living a life that she truly loves. She is 100 percent the happiest, most fulfilled, most passionate about her life that I've ever seen her. She is positively glowing with purpose—no glittery bronzing highlighter necessary. Cara knew what she wanted, despite how shocked everyone had been by her decision. She is fully in flow. She is living her purpose, and no amount of money (or free lip plumpers) could ever come remotely close to comparing to that feeling of contentment. No amount of self-tanner spray for life could ever replace the sense of purpose that comes from living her true calling or purpose.

But it didn't just *happen*. Cara had the guts to go with her gut. She had the balls to decide she wanted a different deal. She had the audacity to follow her inner GPS lady even when everyone else in the car was screaming "Wrong turn!" She knew better. And guess what: as a fellow gutsy gal, so. do. you.

KILLING YOU WITH KINDNESS

Like Cara, if I had listened to my parents, my aunts and uncles, my friends, my boss (the list goes on), and stayed put in Maryland where everyone else thought I belonged, I'm pretty sure I would have stayed lost. I would have stayed restless living a version of my life that I wasn't actually destined to live. It wasn't until I abandoned the "big mistake" external search for answers and tuned into my inner compass that I made a startling discovery: I actually wasn't as lost as I thought. I actually *did* know what I wanted—exactly what I wanted, in fact. And it's my hope that you feel the same about your big life crossroads choices. If your answer is "Yes, but . . . ," we're going to tackle that. If your answer is "Not really," or "I'm not sure," or "I think so," or "I've never really thought about it," it might be time for you to consider dealing yourself a new hand.

Maybe you *like* where you live and you hate California (the "weather tax" is no joke!). Or you already have a sense of purpose in your current job and you don't want to make a massive career shift. Good news! You don't have to. Your biggest opportunity for a life-altering impact comes from finding a way to audaciously reinvent yourself within the realm of your current reality. How? Simple: you decide if you're being the right amount of kind to yourself or killing yourself with your own kindness.

Without cueing up the Roberta Flack song or the Fugees cover, what exactly does that mean?

Well, you've heard the saying, "Kill them with kindness," but what if you're actually being *so* kind (or selfless or empathetic or substitute other applauded adjective here) that you end up slowly crushing yourself one tight smile at a time? What if your thoughtfulness takes so much energy to bring that brightness to others' lives over and over that you're running dangerously low on the reserves needed to keep your own lamp burning? What if your generosity is so all-encompassing that you are attempting to pour the water you need to survive from an empty freaking cup?

See, what really paralyzes us from pulling the trigger on making big moves is our fear, especially as women, of how our actions will affect our people. Now, thinking through how your decision will affect others in a positive or negative light is obviously being a good human. But if doing the right thing is having an over-the-top negative impact on your mental or physical health, are you *sure* it's not actually the wrong thing dressed up in a "Be a good person" graphic T-shirt?

There's another way to deduce whether or not you're sticking with something, someone, or someplace for the right or wrong reasons. And it's something so fundamental, so basic, so primal that we don't even recognize it as one of the top methods our inner GPS lady uses to flag our attention: *sleep.*

If you can't sleep at night or you feel tired no matter how many almond milk lattes you swig, unless you have a newborn baby or puppy, *you* are overindexing on everyone else. An inability to sleep or ever feel "rested" is your subconscious's last-ditch effort to get your attention before you continue on what could be a decidedly ditch-bound direction. You could be actually killing

yourself with too much "kindness" toward your romantic partner, your child, your extended family, your boss, your clients, or
even your dog. And if you're finding yourself currently in the
middle of a situation like one of my dearest friends did, where it's
an exhausting combination of all the things, it's high time for you
and me to sort that shit *out*.

I wish you could meet my friend Kate. Her backstory is that
she's the youngest of a large blended family; her parents divorced
and married a few different partners over the years, and from a
life of constant moving and mayhem, she learned to be a "perfect" go-with-the-flow pleaser. She's her absolute happiest when
she receives positive feedback from her people. This never really
impacted her negatively; in fact, quite the contrary, as she has
more friends than most, though things have changed after she
started a family of her own.

Over the last five years, she has found herself stuck in a
death-by-kindness cycle of trying to make everyone else in her
world *so* happy that at the end of every night even her fingernails
feel exhausted. Now I can hear you thinking, *OK, Erin, we're all
a little tired, so what?* We're not talking "Need a nap at 3 p.m."
or "Why I am in my jammies at 8 p.m." levels of tired. We're
talking fully caffeinated, midmorning, potentially able to cry on
command. We're talking mind, body, and soul sleep-deprived.

Now, sweet reader, I can hear you defending Kate. Well, she
has a lot of responsibilities: What do you expect? And look, *far*
be it from me to ever weigh in on any parent on the planet with
any emotion other than sheer awe, admiration, and respect. Full
stop. You are doing the Lord's work on a level that those of us

who are not parents cannot ever comprehend, and we honor you with endless gratitude. Thank you for being so selfless in raising the next generation of tiny humans.

Yet spending a recent weekend with Kate in her home and seeing everyone tell her to jump and hearing her ask "How high?" over and over again—it was positively heartbreaking. So over a third glass of wine (and by the way, in the 15 years I've known Kate, she had never been a big drinker), once everyone was (finally) asleep, she had the big, messy boo-hoo. And she's one of those friends who when they cry, your heart shatters into a million pieces because they are always everyone else's cheerleader. She started letting out a torrent of troubles, listing a million things she hadn't done in ages; and when she got down to the semicrazy ones like rearranging old basement closets, I interrupted with the aggressive "stop" hand and asked her what was her number one. After a big pull from her Petit Verdot, she expressed, "Sweating. I have to move my body. I have to work out. It makes me feel sane. But I just don't have the energy. Or the time."

So, right there, the two of us mapped out a plan that involved a rocket-ship-level mission strategy consisting of outsourcing, saying no, and committing to at least three workouts a week with monetary consequences for accountability. A few months later, to Kate's credit, she stuck to our pact. Did it take some adjusting from her household crew who were used to having Kate waiting on them hand and foot, like an on-demand superhero? Yep. Did they like it at first? Nope. Do they like it now? Still nope. But are they more than fine picking up some of the slack and sharing responsibilities? Heck yes. And has Kate's decision to prioritize her workouts over the protests of her dependents infused her life with the energy she needs to show up as her best self to all? You know the answer to this one, friend.

Sometimes what we need is *not* a revolutionary reset; sometimes what we need is just small, incremental deal-changers to improve our happiness deposits and keep our bodies, minds, and hearts in the black. Most of the time, staying out of the red danger zone doesn't require a cross-country move or a complete career reinvention; sometimes just a slight reallocation of time and energy can be enough to remove the sarcasm from our versions of "just living the dream."

DOUBLE DOWN ON YOUR DIFFERENT

As you're evaluating where you invest your BDE (Big Deal Energy), maybe you feel like in this particular season you don't have the option to clear a new path for yourself. Maybe your personal responsibilities are making your professional options seem limited. If so, surprisingly enough, you are actually in the perfect place for a little audacious reset. The most powerful way to reboot your current role or actualize your dream one within your existing set of circumstances is to remember that thing everyone always asks you: "How did you *do* that?" And when people do ask you that, you look at them like they are nuts because can't everyone do that thing? Pay attention to what comes easily to *you*, that you do differently from other people, that talent or skill that constantly triggers their admiration. This is the most surefire way to define what type of deal might just be your winning hand if you played it right. No matter what you are facing down right now in your role at work or at home, there is almost always a surprising strategy or solution that only your Big Deal self can see.

Let me introduce you to my friend Sarge. (Sarge is short for Sergeant. Her real name is Ashley. Other nicknames include Maneater and Big Momma, and lest you conjure up an inaccurate visual, she's barely five feet tall.) Anyway, Sarge is one of those people who stomps authoritatively through life, fearlessly commands the room, bosses people around (but in a hilarious, appreciated way), and just always seems to have all the answers. Sarge is the friend in your life that you bring your totally tangled-up favorite necklace to and she hands it back to you, tangle-free, just in time for happy hour. It's likely that you know a Sarge, and if you don't, well, then it's likely you are a Sarge.

I'll never forget when she started a corporate sales job and within two years she was outearning the men on her team 15 years her senior, was driving a BMW, and had purchased her own home at the ripe old age of 25. How? Sarge knew she was a Big Deal, and she didn't really give a rat's bum whether anyone else agreed with this belief. She constantly, audaciously looked for ways not to try and be better than the rest of the team, but to discover how she could be different. Sarge didn't try to one-up what everyone else was doing, instead she kept her eyes on her own paper and brainstormed something so outlandish, so untapped, so "that will never work"—that it ended up being friggin' brilliant. While the other salespeople were chasing down the same classic categories of clients from real estate to healthcare to retail, Sarge took a minute to look inside and ask what she had to offer that none of these midforties, SportsCenter-obsessed, suburban dads did not.

One day, she was driving in Baltimore City in her Beamer past yet another block-long megachurch when the idea struck her like Old Testament lightning. Every business in the city that wanted to attract new customers was already being called on by a dozen Tahoe-driving dads named Steve. But what about these massive churches? Surely, they could also use advertising to attract new attendees. As the sister of a pastor and someone who considered herself to be fairly spiritual, she knew that the mega-churches were run not so differently from lay businesses. Sure, the branding was more "saving souls" than "saving money," but the need to spread awareness at scale was the same.

Naturally, when Sarge pitched this idea to her then-bosses, they laughed at her. And naturally, because Sarge knew she was a Big Deal, she audaciously ignored them and began cold calling and knocking on the doors of Baltimore's biggest churches. This radically different approach meant that as the only television rep in the city approaching houses of worship for advertising and she quickly amassed her own big book of business while also help-ing connect the people of Baltimore with an even more helpful type of Big Book. She was helping spread a message she believed in and also used her commissions to buy a home in the city. Let's just say SportsCenter Steve wasn't laughing at her anymore.

But discovering *your* "different" isn't just something that can be done when you're at the height of a corporate career. Sarge resurrected this same differentiating technique years later, when she started her own family. She had listened to one too many of her "have it all" working mom friends who struggled with the constant feeling of letting someone down, whether it was kids or clients. The "balance" she observed seemed tough to strike and just personally didn't appeal to her. She decided that she didn't want to be a working mom who never saw her kids or a stay-at-home mom without a professional outlet to leverage her hard-earned, sales skill set. She "wanted it all," but without the pervasive "mom guilt" many of her corporate friends were struggling with. So again, she hit the drawing board and asked herself: Where is option three? Where is the opportunity that most people miss? Is there a different way that I can "have it all?"

She found a work-from-home opportunity, began her own at-home business selling wellness products, and 10 years later, she manages her own independent sales team, is a fully hands-on 24/7 mom, and is on track to achieve her goal of giving her husband the freedom to retire earlier than expected. So what about *your* option three? What option might you not even be considering because it's maybe a little more offbeat than the usual paths most taken? Let's roll up our sleeves, borrow a page out of Sarge's playbook, and figure out how you can stop trying to be perfect or the best and start discovering your "different." Let's deal yourself a better hand.

⇉ BIG DEAL DIARY ⇇

Here's where the work comes in and I ask you to *please* consider evolving from passive reader to active writer by keeping a Big Deal Diary. The Big Deal Diary is not a time-blocking planner, nor is it a goal-setting journal. Just like when you were young, your diary is quite simply a safe space for the most private of feelings. Writing here is a small practice at the end of each chapter where you commit to exchanging a few minutes of scroll time for a few moments of *soul* time. This diary of free-flowing emotions (versus to-do lists and time management) could also be the difference between just reading the ideas in this book *and* actually creating positive and lasting change in your life.

While we all know the journaling craze is Romans and Jesus and Stoics age-old, there's a reason for pen-to-paper self-philosophizing's longevity. A new brain imaging study published by UCLA psychologists in 2017 found that putting our feelings into words on paper actually produces therapeutic effects in the brain. They discovered that writing down our emotions can actually increase cognitive function, improve anxiety, and make sadness, anger, and pain less intense.

So let's do this together. Grab a notebook or some Post-it® notes, or if you're looking to treat yourself, head over to bigdeal.erinking.com and order your own official Big Deal Diary.

As you read through the following questions, listen to yourself for the first answers that come to mind. Write your answers freely, without judging, for as long as you feel like. Some days you might write so much it feels like you're completing a college dissertation you never did get around to finishing; another day you might just write one big wise power word that should be etched onto a rock. Either way, now is the time for all your beautiful honesty to flow freely, without judgment, for only you to see:

✳ Do you feel like you have expectations for yourself or your life that aren't currently being met? Or aren't being met in the way that you would like? If not, *yay*! If so, what are they?

✳ Do you feel like other people have expectations about you or your life that aren't being met? If not, *yay*! If so, what are they?

✳ Do you feel the urgency to "figure it out now"? If so, do you feel like that because *you* feel like that or because someone else is influencing you? Or maybe both?

✳ Do you feel like you know what you want (remember those loud, GPS-lady urges) that you feel like you "can't" or "shouldn't" act on because of how someone else might react? What are those things? What kind of reactions might they prompt from whom? (Or if you feel like you don't know what you want, you can write that, too: we'll get to figuring that out later in the book.)

✳ Do you feel like your interactions with the closest 5 to 10 people in your life are generally healthy or unhealthy? *Healthy* meaning after being with them, you feel energized or secure or grateful. *Unhealthy* meaning after being with them, you feel tired, frustrated, or worst of all, indifferent.
List your top 5 people and give each one a number from 1 to 10, with 1 being super-unhealthy and 10 being überhealthy. Next to anyone under a 7, write down why you categorized the person as that.

✳ Fill in the blank: Someday, I'd love to

_____ .

✳ Describe a time in the past when you felt really happy. Who were you with? What were you doing?

✳ Whom do you appreciate most in your life right now? Why?

✳ Whom in your life has opinions about you that maybe should hold less weight with you? In other words, is there perhaps someone in your life who, with all due respect and love, can kiss your audacity?

Reread your answers to the previous questions. Simply allow yourself to feel the emotions you feel for each one. Don't judge how you feel or skip over this part; just pay attention to how you feel in your heart as you read through each one, line by line. Later, in future end-of-chapter work, we'll ease into action steps based on your writings. But for now, sit with your feelings. When you start to discount them or rationalize them, try as best you can not to "put" them somewhere. Can you just observe them for what they are? Which one of your answers made you get a lump in your throat, or made your eyes fill up, or made you bite your lip? Which one turned you into the clenched-teeth emoji face? Circle or highlight that one. We'll come back to that later. And in case no one has told you yet today, nice work, you Big Deal you.

#BIGDEALBOOK

CHAPTER 2

FACE YOUR FAKE NEWS FEARS

As women, let's be real; many of us have sadly been known to fake at least one thing in our day. (Which, by the way, while it might protect your partner's ego in the short term, does no one any favors long term. #ScrewThat.)

On the other hand, there's one thing most of us have never faked: our fear of failure. We fear failing when it comes to the massively vital components of our lives, like our goals and our relationships. We fear failing when it comes to the teeny minuscule components of our lives, like our outfits and Instagram captions.

Despite our daily dominating doubts, we *also* all know at least one person in our life who somehow seems impervious to this fear of failure. Someone who is somehow missing the jittery gene. This person seems bulletproof. Badass. Unafraid (for the most part) of the world saying "Oh no, girl." In writing this book, I grilled the grittiest gals I know on exactly *how* they got to be like that. *How* were they so efficient at keeping their anxiety and worries at bay? And I came in *hot*. I wasn't going to settle for workouts or wine or woo-woo meditation. I wanted the *real* answers, no matter how nonsexy they might be. And my suspicions (like yours perhaps!) proved correct. Every single powerhouse gal ultimately landed on some nonmagic bullet version of this: They were simply better at being brave because they had failed *the most*. Their armor was forged from the sheer quantity *and* quality of their failures. The secret to their strength stemmed from learning with intention as their wounds of failure healed into their scars of success. And at the end of our conversations (many of which you can listen to on my podcast, *Highlights with Erin King*), almost every single gal flipped the script on me and told me to think about what I'd already experienced and subsequently accomplished. Which, of course, I instantly brushed off with a "yeah, yeah, whatever" vibe.

Here's where I need to pause and ask you something: why is it that as women, we are so deeply programmed to discount our own stories? Why did it take *a dozen* of my sheroes to tell me that my story matters before I actually began to believe them? How many times are we going to disregard our anecdotes with the classic audacity asphyxiator: "Oh yes, but it's not like I've done [*insert cooler, more badass person or story here*]." *Yes*, there is always someone who has made a much "larger" impact than you, but there are also those who have never even *tried* or come close to the impact of *your* experience. We must become better at internalizing the fact that our memoirs *matter*.

There is no scarcity when it comes to our most sacred stories. Her story and your story and my story and your other story can *all* take up residence within the success story sanctuary. Yes, our individual adventures of success and failure, of courage and fear, may have had different impacts, but they are all of equal importance. While I don't know your failure fables (yet), with the encouragement of my fellow sisters and, I hope, the "go-on" nod from you, here's mine.

I started not one but *two epic-fail* businesses. I'm not talking about my own little side hustle that didn't pan out and was kind of embarrassing when I had to update my LinkedIn with my plan B backup job. I'm talking about failures of truly *epic proportions*: I'm talking about the fancy, oceanfront Laguna Beach office with a heart-attack-inducing monthly rent and a dozen W-2 employees. I'm talking about the six figures of overhead in the form of payroll and more every month. I'm talking about the unhappy investors who pulled out of their contracts. I started, ran, and closed down two fiscally unsustainable and unsuccessful companies—and it *totally sucked.*

After I walked away from my first venture, Jump Digital Media, it took me years to dig out of my personal $70,000 credit-card debt working at a nine-to-five corporate cubicle job playing stupid office politics and barely enduring a monotonous, horrendous *Groundhog Day* existence (sooooo much "touching base"). My professional life, for a few years, was, to be California concise, a total bummer. I *lived* for the weekends. Sunday Scaries to the max. At 4:59 on a Friday I made a beeline for the first barstool I could find at Yard House for a cold beer to help me forget that I was spending most of my precious life submerged in spreadsheets. A pint later I would inevitably begin face-blasting some poor innocent guy who didn't ask and didn't care *at all* about how I used to be a super-cool entrepreneur. It was the most unfulfilled (and annoying) I've ever been in my life.

So let's take a quick flashback to where we started with our tampon talk in the Introduction. I'm not afraid to tell you that, just like there's more to a Disney movie after it ends with everyone living happily ever after, there's more to the story that you weren't exactly shown. There's a reason *Ariel and Prince Eric: After the Marriage* doesn't exist. Ariel has buyer's remorse and wants to be a mermaid again, so she and Ursula slug drinks down by the dock while reminiscing about how cool life was like "Unda da Sea." Or something like that. In real life, my PMS.com "not so happily ever after" ending went something like this.

After getting the backing of Todd and the Tan Tampon Dudes, my team and I spent months creating the perfect "tampon fairy" brand. (Magically delivered monthly for just $15!) We designed packaging, websites, ads, and emails. We became experts on FDA regulations and Chinese supply-chain shipping policies. My friend Kylee and I drove to the Port of Long Beach at 5 a.m. to pick up tampon shipments that had arrived by boat from Asia. We learned the extremely complex world of e-commerce inventory management. We ruminated on how to maximize margins on an already very inexpensive, highly accessible product controlled by legacy brand giants. *Forbes* wrote an article on us, and as Dollar Shave Club had just been bought by Unilever for $1 billion, I had all intentions of replicating that success in the women's healthcare space.

But that's not what happened. Not. At. All.

34

Even though I thought it was a genius idea (because I never had tampons on hand when I needed them), the actuality was a big, fat *nope*! Turns out, most women are just responsible adults who pick them up at the grocery store, like normal people. Not a Big Deal, if you will. And for women who were open to the idea, it was really, really tough to convince them to abandon the brands they had trusted since back when Nirvana was on the radio. We ran every ad campaign. Deployed every social media strategy. We sank crazy amounts of capital into public relations. We recruited influencers and sent emails, and even though we had about 20,000 women subscribe, about 18 months into the venture, all financial signs were pointing to a big, fat failure. (Startup side note: Is your big idea actually solving a seriously severe problem? Is your concept a nice-to-have or a *need*-to-have? Those answers are likely the difference between excruciating pain and extraordinary profits.)

As our fiscal runway got shorter and shorter (and my stress levels skyrocketed higher and higher), I finally bit the bullet and scheduled a meeting in that same beautiful Pacific Ocean conference room where we had begun. Except it didn't look as packed with promise as the first time I was there. It felt more like a funeral home where I would be laid to rest on that beautiful long marble table. Surrounded, of course, by our remaining unsold, massive inventory of Chinese-manufactured tampons.

The investors who had said they bet "on the jockey, not the horse"—aka "me, not the idea"—listened to me eat a massive poo sandwich, as I admitted straight up that I had failed. The jockey had run this horse into the ground. It was humiliating. It was nauseating. It was the mother-of-all-confidence erasers.

The logistics involved in shutting down PMS.com felt like a never-ending messy divorce. I lost former dear friends who had become disgruntled employees in legal battles. I had to negotiate my way out of ironclad supplier contracts. (The ones in Chinese were particularly challenging.) I lost face in our small, everyone-knows-everyone beach town.

The worst part? I lost all faith in myself because my fear of failure had come to fruition. And it turns out, the reason that we fear failure so ferociously is because when you fail on a large scale and face-plant with no one to blame but yourself, it is horrendous. Professionally, it paralyzed me. For months and months, my legit fiscal failure froze me from doing anything but wallowing in my self-pity, self-flagellation, and real self-hatred. For weeks, I was so haunted by my defeat that I started losing huge clumps of hair in the shower. I would wake up in the middle of the night in a full-body sweat, somewhere strange in my house after sleepwalking during night terrors. In an extreme twist of irony, the former failed CEO of PMS.com was *so* afflicted by anguish that I actually stopped getting my period for a few months!

One day, after drinking too much red wine, eating an *entire* bucket of Trader Joe's peanut butter cups, and crying my mascara'd eyes out for hours, I stared into the bathroom mirror like a complete psycho and said out loud, "You are an absolute loser." This doesn't sound that dramatic as I'm writing it here now, and it's not like I was actually physically harming myself or anything, but for a pretty baseline positive person, it scared the hell out of me for two reasons: (1) I was talking to myself out loud in a mirror, and (2) I was being downright malicious about it.

Why the vile self-talk? *Because I was totally terrified.* Sure, we're all afraid of something. Yes, cancer, snakes, and the regretful return of nineties fashion like scrunchies, fanny packs, and bike shorts are frightening, to be sure. But above all, it's those look-in-the-mirror moments that alarm us to the deepest degree. This is why we fear *all* the Ghosts of Failure: our past failures, our current failures, and our future failures. We fear letting our failures direct our choices. We fear repeating mistakes, falling short of our own or others' expectations, botching the job, losing the money, missing out on the best option, or having regrets. We fear the repercussions of our choices. We fear judgment. We fear punishment. We fear staying stuck in analysis paralysis. We fear not achieving our perfectionist fantasies. We fear that we just aren't enough. We fear the no. Sometimes we even fear that we aren't being fearful enough! Many of us have been groomed to think of fear as a zero-sum situation: it's you or the fear. If that's true, then the reality is that there's no way to successfully coexist with it, right?

Tell me something: when was the last time your fear of failure held you back from making a move? Was it one of those situations where you really wanted to say something to someone that everyone else is scared to? Or maybe it was one of those times where no matter how much you analyzed something to death, you knew there was actually no other way to do it besides jumping out of the plane and pulling the ripcord—even when people (whose opinions matter to you) would think you're insane? Or maybe it was that time you knew exactly what you needed to do or walk away from, but you were paralyzed with anxiety that it had the potential to trigger massive disappointment or judgment (or both) from someone you love? And while you may have avoided letting that one person down, in the process, you let yourself down. So, really, you still failed anyway! *Ugh*. Is it any wonder something this shitty is so powerfully paralyzing?

Here's the thing: our fear of failure (especially as women) far too often comes not just from an objective standpoint, but from a subjective standpoint via the opinions of others. Now, I'm certainly not going to dispense the ridiculous notion that you "shouldn't care what anyone thinks about you" because (1) it will never actually happen unless (2) you become a ragingly self-centered narcissist nightmare of a human. If we never took our truth-tellers two cents to help us get back on course when we lose our way, we'd be lost in the Kanye West woods of life. We all have situations where people we love have let us know that we're riding the Hot Mess Express—and thank goodness they did! But distinguishing between "looking out for you" reactions and "holding you back" reactions is where things morph into murkier waters.

See, there is something about your fear that is *so critical* to really realize, and fully grasping this fact has been the catalyst for Big Deal courage in my life like nothing else.

You probably know that what holds you back from doing *the thing* is that, on some level, you're afraid of people you care about reacting negatively to it, yes? But that's not really what you're afraid of. Not deep down. What you're really afraid of (and this is something that is tough for any of us to admit) is not that they're rejecting what you're doing. It's that what they're *really* doing is rejecting *you*. You might fear them rejecting who you are as a friend, a family member, a colleague, or a lover. You fear them rejecting you as a *human*. In fact, if I may come in super-hot with this, you are probably *so* afraid that the people you love (and sometimes even people you don't know) will reject who you are at your core, that it's the number one thing keeping you scared, stuck, and staying in line *right now*. Even if you know better. Because your heart always trumps your head. And who would ever want someone you love to not love you back? For some of us, we'd rather be dead! (A tad dramatic, but you're tracking with me, right?) I can honestly say that much of my fear after my business failures stemmed from this maddening mindset.

See, the truth is (and we all know this to be true) that reactions are just reflections. People's reactions to you are just a reflection of how your big, bold, audacious move made them feel. Or what it made them reflect on in their own life. Maybe your Big Deal move forced them to view a version of themselves in a mirror that they thought they had nice and covered up. Or that they perceive as being a small deal reflection by comparison.

This is why *big changes* trigger *big reactions*. And the more massive your move, the more the world can't help but match it with a massive response. If what you are doing isn't significant, isn't a game-changer, isn't really that big a deal, people's reactions won't be, either. So if you're hell-bent and determined to retain your relationships in the "happy days, frictionless, good times zone," fabulous! But just know that the flip side is you're also staying still, and only you can know if that stillness is safe or suffocating.

Big changes trigger big reactions. And the more massive your move, the more the world can't help but match it with a massive response.

So the question is: What if you reprogrammed the way your brain classifies big, oftentimes negative or less-than-comfortable, reactions? What if you rewired your mind to process a big scary reaction as a green light, instead of a red one? What would happen in your life if you transformed the momentum-stalling "No, girl" into a momentum-igniting "Go, girl!"?

Someone's objection to your decision isn't necessarily a rejection of who you are. Because doing and being aren't the same. Have you ever known a good person to do a bad thing? Or a bad person to do a good thing? Not to get down on Kanye again, but you can love the song "Stronger" as your go-to pump-up anthem without Kanye being your go-to person in terms of mentors or advice dispensers. And the same goes for you: your people can love you without loving your choices. The people who love you the most might not love those choices *right away*, but if they're truly your people, they will eventually.

After I moved to California, my dad finally came back around (a decade after threatening to cut me out of his will). He commended me on my choices. His "No, girl" finally became a "Go, girl!" but only because I chased down my dream in spite of his rejection. Which really *really* sucked at the time, but was really *really* worth it in the long run. Worth it even after my failed businesses—because my failure wounds healed into success scars, just like yours have, will soon, or will someday, but only if you have the Big Deal courage to keep going in the direction you know you must.

Once you can really realize this deep down in your heart of hearts, you'll also understand that many of the fears that

40

freeze you from going forward are the fakest of fake news. And every time you stutter-step on your path to where you know you were destined to travel, that's just you accidentally taking the fake news clickbait. You're unintentionally sending stupid spam right to your sweet soul. And if, for some reason, it's not? That that person sees your actions and doesn't love you? Well, is that someone you really want in your life anyway? Or is that someone who can just kiss your audacity? Because if that person doesn't know that you're kind of a Big Deal, well, that's just simply not your problem.

UNPACKING YOUR FAKE NEWS FEARS

You might raise seven figures of capital for a startup company (or you might start a new job/venture/side hustle) and fall flat on your freaking face. You might do it in front of a lot of people who laughed at you from the start. You might move (back) across the country for the "love of your life" and then break up a year later. You might lose your best friend in a tragic jet-skiing accident. You might be told one day that you or someone you love has a health issue that a few Advil cannot solve. You might lose your eight-month-old puppy to a freak car accident even though you were a helicopter dog mom who was obsessed with protecting your fur baby from that exact fate. These are my dark stories, and you have yours, and there's nothing we can do about fearing life's scariest shit because it is real and it can happen.

While this may be true, fear is also the thing that keeps us from getting in elevators with sketchy men. Fear is what motivates us to save our money for a rainy day. But it's also true that the majority of the things we fear going wrong are typically *not* quite so life shattering. It's more likely that our everyday fears are either (1) not going to happen or (2) not going to impact us in the devastatingly negative way that we conjure a false future narrative about. (At least in the end.) It's highly likely that your fears holding you back right now are *fake freaking news*.

So let's unpack some of the most common fake news fears, one at a time. They are ranked in order from all-time most fake to the still-pretty-freaking fake. These fears come to you straight from the brave DMs I've received packed full of fake news loops that some of my online friends still subscribe to even when they know (just like you do) that they should opt out and remove themselves from such a spammy list.

FEAR THAT YOU'LL SCREW UP

Maybe you're afraid that you'll royally screw something up. Let's be clear: unless you are perfect, screwing something up is a *when*, not an *if*. Your fear of screwing up is likely stemming from your childhood, like the first time you knocked over an open gallon of milk all over your mother's immaculate floor mere hours after she had spent an hour on her hands and knees making it shine. Hell hath no fury like a a mother whose kitchen floor was made messy back in the day growing up in our house. Maybe you're afraid you're not ready to take on a leadership role, or launch a new venture, or accept an unprecedented level of responsibility because *what if you screw it up?*

Rejoin me back in my horror movie bathroom scene of mascara down the face and peanut butter cup crumbles accentuating my red wine–stained teeth. The morning after I went mad, I woke up in my loser bed, brushed my loser teeth, and dragged my loser butt to the couch. With my head in my hands, I knew I had to call in some backup before I kept spiraling toward Mayor of Crazy Town (population one).

I asked one of my best friends (who is also a business mentor of sorts) to join me for a beach walk. Staring listlessly at the water, I worked myself up into a frenzy of fears and tears about how I was completely lost, how I hated life and didn't know myself anymore, and how I was falling apart (noticing a trend here? You're not alone!) when suddenly she stopped and grabbed me by the arms: "Hey! *Hey!* Look at me! *You* are not your *business*! You are still Erin, who likes to laugh and drink wine—although maybe you should drink a little less of it these days—but regardless, you are a dear friend! You are there for people when they need you. You are fun and kind and smart. The tampon fairies may be dead, but you're not! *You* are successful with or without the damn *bloody* business!"

And with that horrendous pun, after a huge pause, for the first time in *months*, I burst into laughter. Well, not exactly laughter, but that ugly cry-laugh combo when all the failure feels are bursting forth like water from a fire hydrant. In that ugly cry-laugh moment, finally, after months of agony, the wind and the waves began to carry the most intense sadness away, out to sea. My perspective began to realign, not instantly, but the cracks of light had begun to shine through the darkness.

Whatever failure you've experienced in the past or whatever failure you fear might happen in the future, *you* are not your failure. You are not your business. Your business is not you. These are two separate entities. They belong in two different buckets. I realized that "successful human me" could fully coexist with "unsuccessful CEO me." And the same goes for you. Have you ever noticed that a lot of men are excellent at immediately pointing to *what* went wrong, not *who*? It was the wrong timing, the wrong market, the wrong positioning. No matter what the specifics are, they find ways to assign blame to *external factors*. They certainly don't consider that what went wrong bears any implication on their awesomeness as humans. They are able to separate themselves from what they do with crafty compartmentalization. And it's high time we, as women, become better at doing the same.

Whatever failure you've experienced in the past or whatever failure you fear might happen in the future, you are not your failure.

Now, I realize that sounds easier said than done. Have you ever met those people who underplay how paralyzing fear can be and spout inane platitudes like, "Just throw away your fears!"

What? Where? There's been an official fear trash can this whole time? Where is this elusive, magical fear trash can? Can I get it at Ikea? Did I have one and accidentally Marie-Kondo'd it because "fear" and "joy" are polar opposites?

If you're someone who is so passionate about what you do, who defines yourself by your wins, who lives, eats, breathes, and sleeps your business, your family, your art, or your cause, when you come up short, there will be a mourning period. Like death, it might take you four full calendar seasons of grieving. It certainly took me at least that long. There's no way for any of us to engineer or rush our own cathartic super-moments where the salt water from your face finds its way into the salt water of the ocean. All we can do is be intentional about opening the space for it to occur. And it's only until our failure wounds begin to scab that we can start to see the beginning of our success scars.

The truth about my failure catharsis is it was only after I was able to separate *me* from *my failure* that I was able to discover the pearl left behind. And this pearl changed my entire life. So as I've said, I wasn't exactly marvelous at managing overseas teams or operations of a digital subscription service, but one thing I had managed not to screw up was cultivating a huge online community of millions of women. Women who had come together on PMS.com's Facebook page (which you can still see today) to connect over a previously taboo topic. Our little page became the internet's largest space at that time for "period joke" laughter and "why aren't there more scientific studies on this topic" frustration. I discovered my real superpower was creating camaraderie by nurturing community. But I could only see this once I released all the failure feels. And when I did, I discovered my "third time is a charm," finally fiscally successful venture: creating social media communities for clients via my current business—Socialite Agency. Within the dumpster fire of PMS.com arose the phoenix of Socialite Agency, which finally yielded the monetary success I had been searching for. And I never would have gotten there had I stayed on the couch crushing peanut butter cups—as tempting a lifestyle as that sounds.

Until you release your failure feels, it's impossible to see your good, harness your skills, and unlock your success potential when you're shrouding it in Small Deal Energy! I know that you know you already have what it takes to march boldly toward your dream destiny. But you can't activate it if you can't see it.

Only because of the vital "failure" of not one but two of my own early businesses—Jump Digital Media and PMS.com—could I create the success of Socialite. I went from mean mirror smack-talking to running social media for the Oscars in Hollywood, the US Navy at the Pentagon, and dozens more of the world's biggest brands. Those experiences then led to writing books, coaching, and speaking—and my life has *never* been the same! If I could send my failures a massive, handwritten thank you note with a cold magnum of bubbly, I would.

So please hear me here: almost always, rock-bottom rocks. You might know the Rascal Flatts song "Bless the Broken Road." Whatever broken road you're walking, *keep going*. Your "screwups" are just cue-ups for your most audaciously successful destiny to unfold.

Your "screw-ups" are just cue-ups for your most audaciously successful destiny to unfold.

#BIGDEALBOOK

FEAR THAT YOU'LL LOOK STUPID

Sarah Jessica Parker tricked many of us into believing that designer high heels were life-changing, fabulous, and the secret to real happiness. And maybe for you, they are. If you are a heel lover, with all due respect to both you and Carrie, yay for you, but I vehemently disagree. Sure, even though my massive calves do look *slightly* slimmer in a pair of absurdly pricy nude heels, after five minutes of tottering around like a kid playing dress-up, let's just say my dogs are barking. I'm just more of a jeans-and-sneakers surfer gal, and no matter how many years I forced myself to wear heels working with my corporate clients, I still never made peace with my loathing for them. So for *years* I carried the dreaded heels at every conference, to and from each stage, to and from every meeting, to and from every airport like designer ball-and-chain spikes.

One day, I was scrolling Instagram backstage before my opening keynote for a highly conservative corporate sales meeting when I saw a post from my friend Brian Fanzo challenging his followers to try something they were truly afraid to do even for fear of looking stupid. He ended it with "I dare you—today—to walk your most authentic walk."

Just talking about walking authentically propelled me to fantasize about the moment 90 minutes later when I could slip back into my beloved sneakers. Unless . . . what if . . . I dared to just wear my sneakers onstage? With my businessy dress? OK, before we go any further—*yes*, I am fully aware that this is likely an eye-rolling "basic brave" moment. I realize that this is not anywhere in the stratosphere of the universe of big brave. I understand that wearing sneakers on stage is maybe, just maybe, *slightly* less heroic than, say, Malala fighting off the Taliban. Or Bethany Hamilton going back to surfing with only one arm after a shark attack took her other arm. Or other everyday sheroes who stand up to racism, other kinds of discrimination, assault, trauma, and other truly admirable, astonishing, inspiring levels of heroism. I get that daring to wear sneakers onstage is not remotely big brave, but in that moment, in the context of that corporate event, it registered on my little wimpy scale as basic medium brave. And for *most* of us, dear reader, basic medium brave is the most easily accessible bravery gym you can visit to put in your reps so that when you find yourself in your own big brave moment—you're prepared enough to prevail.

So how do you know if the universe is presenting you with a chance to be medium brave? You'll know if you answer yes to any of the following questions: Did your heart race? Did you start to sweat through your Spanx? Did your eyes dart around? Did your inner monologue start to backseat-bicker? If so, you were looking a medium brave moment directly in its defiant face. Back to my majorly basic, medium brave moment:

I remember experiencing all of the above-listed symptoms, plus my hands were uncontrollably shaking at the mere thought of wearing casual sneakers at this highly judgy, tough-crowd, extremely buttoned-up old-school corporate event. I'm already a privileged woman under 40, who loves her job and her life, and for that reason alone the audience does *not* want to like me from the moment I take one step onto that platform. But that's the package I come in, and the truth is that anytime you have a physical reaction to doing something like that—just like when other people react to you in a big way—it's the most excellent indicator that you have just turned the key and are about to unlock your Big Deal Energy.

I remember going back and forth backstage with only minutes to spare, thinking:

> *What if the client gets mad because she requested business attire?*
>
> *What if the stiff corporate crowd doesn't take me seriously?*
>
> *What if I look like a large-calved linebacker since, while comfortable, these high-tops do cut me off in exactly the wrong place?*
>
> *What if people think I'm trying to be like some cool young hipster that I'm certainly not?*

Then I thought of the worst-case scenario. As a female keynoter, while you're presenting, people typically tweet—a lot—

about your appearance. They love your dress; they hate your dress. Your energy is amazing; your energy is too much. *What if they write mean tweets about the fact that urban black high tops with a suburban preppy pink dress is not a look in any stylebook on the planet?*

As I was pacing backstage, my mind racing with the Crazy Town overanalysis of these absurd deliberations, one of the AV guys walked by and tossed off, "Cool sneaks." Reflexively, I looked back over down at his, and hand to the sky they were the dirtiest pair of Chuck Taylors you could ever imagine. These were Chucks this guy had either been wearing since pre-school or found in a dumpster, or both. "Um, thanks. Yours, too," I returned with the sincerity of a Southerner "blessing your heart." I will *never* forget this guy puffing his chest up, and with the *most confidence* I'd ever seen, he said: "Yeah, I know. Sick, right? I love 'em."

And as he kind of nerd-strutted away, I was hit by something. This is obviously a massive generalization, but for the most part, dudes are fairly unfazed by looking dumb. Or not being stylish enough. They just don't! I'm not wrong here, and I'll prove it. When soccer was shut down in Europe during the pandemic, a contest for the "oldest-looking" former soccer players surfaced online, where competitors would win points for categories like being bald or having yellow teeth. These 50- and 60-year-olds started posting the ugliest photos of themselves online in hopes of being voted the "oldest looking" and winning the competition! Globally, historically, and generationally agnostic: dudes just have this attitude like, *Eff it! I'm the man!* I call it a Dude-itude.

And it's audaciously awesome. And for many of us gals, in many situations, in my opinion we, as a whole, could sure stand to borrow some Dude-itude of our own.

So I used Mr. Chucks' overconfidence in his dumpster kicks. I took a deep breath and instead of walking out in my heels like a perfectly poised, pink-dress beauty pageant contestant, for the first time ever, I *ran* out onto the stage like a gladiator facing down dragons.

And in that medium brave moment, I felt like I had been reborn. My impostor syndrome, formerly protected by power pumps, immediately evaporated. Wearing what made me physically comfortable enabled me to release any anxiety around what the audience might think or do or tweet. Showing up authentically in a way that I felt comfortable authorized me to show up mentally in a way that I'd never been able to access before. I shocked myself by lying down on the stage to act out a story. I could move confidently without being afraid of tripping. I was so relaxed, I had so much fun, and I was so in the moment that not only did the people in the audience *not* judge me the way I had feared, but they gave me the very first standing ovation of my speaking career. Everything I had worried about backstage was all 100 percent *fake news*. Yes, it was just a pair of stupid sneakers. But one teeny, tiny, "So what?" choice ignited a series of events that began to change the trajectory of my entire career. Something as insignificant as a pair of sneaks ignited this momentous shift in my life. Those kicks were a tangible sign that an acceleration of authenticity and an authorization of genuineness were needed, like, yesterday.

If you're also mentally manufacturing moments that haven't happened or imagining how a scenario might play out for the worst, can you remind yourself that you are likely succumbing to fake news mental clickbait? Because not only do things *not* happen the way we fear (like the sneaks), but being audacious enough to own your authenticity, no matter how initially scary it might be, enables an even *more* magical experience to transpire for you. Walking (or running) with the belief that you are already a Big Deal is the fastest gateway to getting more standing ovations on the stage of your life. This experience wasn't about the sneakers; it was about the Big Deal Energy that rocking them unlocked. What could be possible for you if you stepped into your authentic awesomeness with your own pair of sneakers, heels, outfit, or whatever it is for you that makes you feel like the Big Deal that you actually are? I'm over here cheering and applauding with the highest hopes that your answer is not just yes but a resounding *hell yes*!

Now, let's take this talk from offline to online—let's unpack what living in the Digital Age means when it comes to the fear around looking stupid. For starters, take a wild guess who is viewing your social media profiles the most of anyone on the entire internet? Who do you honestly think is examining your carefully curated Instagram, LinkedIn, or Facebook "life résumé"? No, it's not the ex who never got over you. (Well, actually it might be. Once you've dated a Big Deal, it's tough to go back.) But seriously, the answer is *you*. Social data scientists find, time and time again, that the most views on anyone's profile 90 percent of the time (excluding celebrities and influencers) are from the profile owner's *own* account. Think about it . . . have you ever looked at your own Instagram Story, TikTok video, LinkedIn résumé, or Facebook bio and tried to contemplate it through someone else's eyes? No? Are you sure? What about when you meet some really cool people and connect with them online? You've never tried to look at your profile and wonder, just for a little bit, what they might be thinking about you? Uh-huh . . . sure, you haven't.

Here's a truth that you can find either extremely depressing or incredibly liberating: not only is the world not judging you for how "stupid" you may or may not look online; most people in your orbit aren't even thinking about you *at all*. Other than your mom, your grandma, and maybe your bestie, this major lack of other people contemplating you and your choices can be one of the most empowering insights you'll ever embrace. Bear-hug this truth, shake off the ego bruise, and charge forward with a candid answer to this question: What have you been afraid to do, say, or try because you fear looking stupid in front of other people? Or perhaps in front of one particular person? Can you even imagine what might be possible if you chose to focus less on what that person might think (but probably won't!) and more on what your heart desires you to dare to do or try?

Maybe it's something as small, silly, and medium brave as choosing an outfit or footwear that isn't "standard" for the situation you're strutting into but it makes *you* feel that BDE (or at least super-comfy). Maybe it's something heftier like going back to school at an "older" age or picking up a hobby that's typically "for kids." Whether you dream of wearing sneakers when you're supposed to wear heels or traveling the world or being radically real with a client, boss, coworker, or child—*do it*. And when you do grab hold of your audacity, and you do actualize your Big Deal moment, will you share it on Instagram? Because your Big Deal moment deserves a virtual standing ovation. And even better? It will inspire others to lace up for their very own Big Deal moment as well. (Tag me @mrs.erin.king so I can see you in action!)

FEAR THAT YOU'LL ACTUALLY DO THE DANG THING

Personally, I find this is the craziest of the fake news fears because I never really fathomed it could actually be real. The fear of failure I understand sure, but what kind of sadist would fear success? Well it turns out a lot of people have this fear and that not only is our unconscious self-sabotage a *very* real thing; it's sneaky as hell, too.

Have you ever found yourself within reach of that one goal, milestone, promotion, or relationship, and then found yourself tripping up, dragging your feet, or doing something just straight-up *stupid*? My friend Judi Holler *totally* called me out on this once when I was making excuses about my procrastination "problem." I would always joke around saying, "Why do meeting planners always ask for our slide decks *so* far in advance? Don't they understand that the best slides can only be created within one hour of show start time?" She challenged me gently, explaining that procrastination is typically a huge indicator that on some subatomic particle level I was actually fearful of the success that might come with operating from a place of organized calm. She suggested that

I was actually afraid of what I could be capable of if I got my shit together with my time management and took my ability to deliver on time to the next level. She explained that I was terrified of operating without the adrenaline rush of "Will it all get done in time?" that I had been feeding on like some kind of deranged diva. I really used to categorize the notion of being "the one in your own way" as something truly preposterous. Why would we ever do that to ourselves? Why would we ever work *so* hard—only to build a dam stopping up our hard-earned flow of abundance?

Well, as Judi (who is an expert on fear management) explained it to me: Success means change. Success means higher expectations. Success means bigger demands on your time, your mind, and your body. If (and when) you "fail," everyone sees it— even if what people see as failure is only a stepping-stone you needed to lead you to success. And that success forces us to dig deeper than we ever have before, to relocate far away from our hometown comfort zone and examine our flaws and our personal lives under a very revealing, unfiltered, less-than-selfie-perfect spotlight. Maybe you've been feeling scared of success because, deep down, you're scared of the price you might have to pay. Maybe you're scared to trade in your current life that you like for one that is unknown—which you might love more, but you also might not. What if your success changes your relationships that you currently cherish?

What if success changes *you*? And not for the better?

If you really force yourself to examine the answers to these questions, there's actually *some* validity to this fear. But when your desire for a shining future or that Big Deal win is so insatiable that it eclipses the cozy of your mediocre now, the real truth is that your success destiny has sort of already been decided for you. Your internal GPS lady has already determined that you are not a life passenger that can be content riding in coach forever. And until you both discover what's on the other side of that two-sided coin of paralyzing, promising fear, she's going to manically keep bossing you around until you do! The thrill of your dreams transforming into your actual reality is like a self-driving vehicle whose destination has been preprogrammed. The potential you see for your life will ultimately override any ancient fear of success coordinates. Only if, of course, you have the audacity to keep your foot off that brake as you make a hairpin turn on the windiest roads.

What if today you reconditioned your reaction to your most limiting habits or most bogus beliefs? What if you decided to make your fear of success *old* news? What if today you showed the universe how sincerely serious you actually are about smashing your goals? What if you trashed limiting phrases like "I'm trying to," "I'll eventually," or the worst one: "I'm an 'aspiring' xyz"? What if you raised your hand, no matter where you are, and you said three of the most powerful words you can utter: "*I am ready*"?

Do it! Say it with me: *I am ready*! Kick your fake news fears to the curb and invite your audacity to saddle up for the ride, not tomorrow, not on Monday, not in one year, five years, or ten years. *Today*. Success has a price, but you and I both know that *you are ready* and prepared to pay up. And if you still think you aren't ready? You're even more so. Don't fear your new power. Friend it. And fire away.

☀ BIG DEAL DIARY ☀

We've been through a lot this chapter, so let's process it and put it into practice. As you read through the following questions, listen to yourself for the first answers that come to mind for you. Write your answers freely, without judging.

✳ Let's define *real you* versus *role you*. "Role you" can be the role you "play" in your job, your family, your friend group, your community, or whatever area you are finding yourself struggling to break through to the other side of what you know is possible. Let's leave "role you" on the shelf for this exercise and talk about "real you":

- ↺ What are your "real you" values and traits that you possess regardless of where you are or what you are doing?

- ↺ What really matters to you?

- ↺ What are your deathbed nonnegotiables about your life that you know you'll look back on with gratitude that you stuck to? What are some of your unbreakable personal code conditions that you are proud to have honored even in some of the toughest of times?

After you've finished listing these, please read through them, pat yourself on the back, and say "Yay, me!," not for what you've accomplished, but simply for who you are. You deserve to feel good about those values and traits. Feel blessed to have them!

✳ Who are three people in your life that you admire, love, or like a lot?

    ↺ Why do you admire, love, or like them?

    ↺ If you were meeting with them for lunch or coffee, what do you think they would say are your most positive traits?

✳ What are the setbacks you have faced lately? Write them all down. Personal *and* professional. Write them all down. Whatever has kept you up at night, frustrated you, or been playing on the mental-tape repeat loop. Include here if you feel you have failed at anything; it can be big or small.

✳ Read through these setbacks one by one. After you read each one, remind yourself that this is just a temporary problem, one that happens to others. Remind yourself that these setbacks are not a reflection of who you are. Acknowledge if any of these setbacks stem from a place of fear. Maybe tomorrow will be a different story, but that's to deal with tomorrow. Say all or a few of the following affirmations:

    ↺ "Just for today, I am going to get back up and keep going."

ᴄ "Just for today, I am going to push through this pain point."

ᴄ "Just for today, I am going to grit my teeth through this challenge."

Or maybe:

ᴄ "Just for today, I'm going to take a break, because I can rest without quitting."

Whatever you need to maintain momentum, to keep swimming, your only concern is not the rest of the week, the month, the quarter, or in 20 years; your only concern is how you choose to move forward—just for today.

✳ How exactly will you accomplish those affirmations that you chose? Write down one doable move to deal with each one, even if only for today. Smile. Breathe. You've got this.

After you complete each of these journaling exercises, it's time for your audacity mantra. This one may be a hard one, since we've spent time journaling all the things that loom large in our minds as fear-triggering failures.

Use this to create a clean slate, like a sommelier cleansing his or her palate between wines. Get the taste of fear off your tongue, and let's move on to the big, bold, unapologetic Caymus Cab that your life is fermenting into.

Take a mental swirl, sip, and savor as you say it with me:

"I'm kind of a Big Deal."

#BIGDEALBOOK

CHAPTER 3

GHOST YOUR INNER GOOD GIRL

J ust reading that chapter title, you might be thinking, *good girl? Erin, please; I'm a feisty, fearless, hear-me-roar-world kinda gal*. And, *yes*, you are. As am I, as are my dearest girlfriends, and likely yours as well. You, me, our friends: we're all cut from the same kickass cloth. *And* I'll never forget the day when one of my dynamo gal pals enlightened me to the reality that even the most audacious among us harbor a sneaky inner good girl, and one that goes way beyond just seeking grown-up gold star stickers.

It was a sunny Sunday morning, and the air smelled like that odd signature combo of refreshing salt and stinky seaweed that permeates Laguna Beach every spring. My girlfriend Sienna and I were meeting for brunch where, as we were catching up, she revealed that she had recently scored a massive win at work. Naturally, two glasses of the fanciest champagne on the menu were ordered to toast her success. As we took our first sip, a true travesty transpired. Instead of a decadent symphony of firework bubbles, the champagne had fallen flat. So Sienna motioned for the waiter and politely requested that a new bottle be opened and sent back the glasses without a second thought. I must have accidentally winced as she did this, because she narrowed her perfectly microbladed brows at me. "What?" she queried. As I hemmed and hawed and tried to change the subject, she wouldn't let me off so easily. Eventually, she dragged out the pathetic truth. Yours truly, the same gal who had founded multiple companies, who spoke in front of tens of thousands of people in stadiums, was *nervous* sending back subpar bubbly?! "Why" she asked incredulously. And here's the anticlimactic, extremely embarrassing pathetic truth: I didn't really have a specific answer. It just felt . . . not allowed. Not OK. *Bad* in some way that I couldn't even articulate rationally. And *that* was the moment when I realized that even you and I and our marvelous friends, those of us who step into the world and take up space and move mountains on the regular, are *still* inherently imprinted with the standards of a society that has taught us the sanctity of being a "good girl."

It was shocking to realize that if I, a grown ass woman who has every right to politely request a fresh bottle of bubbly, felt a knee-jerk hesitation, who else in the world might be unintentionally retaining this "good-girl" programming as well?

So maybe you read that and thought, *Nah, I have no problem sending something back at a restaurant,* but what if there are other shadowy corners where your inner good girl is secretly still alive and well? No matter how much of a Big Deal babe you are, if you answer "Uh, yes," "Slightly sort of," or "Well, just that *one* time" to any of the following 10 questions, the answer is probably (unfortunately) yes:

1. Have you ever been praised for an accomplishment and downplayed it? When someone says to you "Congrats, you totally killed it," have you ever responded with something like, "Well, it was a team effort," "Thanks to so-and-so for helping me," or "It was hard work but also a lot of luck!"? Or have you ever tried to flip it and reverse-compliment the other person to take the spotlight off you: "Well, look who's talking; you're the one who did xyz!"?

2. Have you ever been in a meeting or important discussion and changed or "softened up" your position when you felt people disagreeing with you? Or pretended to kind of agree with something *major* that you didn't really?

3. Have you ever pretended to know what someone was talking about when you didn't?

4. Do you find yourself saying "sorry" often? (And not in the British way of "Can you repeat yourself"?)

5. Have you ever found yourself doing things often that you really want to say no to?

6. Have you ever excessively or accidentally fished for compliments from those you love?

7. Have you ever described yourself as an "aspiring" or "wannabe" something? Like an aspiring author, aspiring performer, wannabe entrepreneur, wannabe chef, and so on? Or called something a "little hobby" when it's something you actually want or plan to make your full-time focus?

8. Have you ever wanted something but been afraid, embarrassed, or ashamed to tell your friends or family about it? Have you ever stopped talking about something you dream about because you don't want to seem braggadocious or crazy?

9. Have you ever had someone praise you or award you in some way, and you felt embarrassed? Maybe you dropped your gaze, shook your head a little, waved the praise away, or felt your cheeks go warm?

10. Have you ever given up on chasing something down or igniting an initiative because you couldn't persuade one person out of several who said *yes* to get onboard with your idea?

So as they say on the socials: Are you feeling personally attacked RN?*

---

* Where RN means "right now." For gray-haired old millennials like myself, this doesn't mean someone is assaulting you, but it's a lighthearted way of saying you relate hard core (*right now*) to what someone just said. Thank you to that 22-year-old who came up to me after my keynote at a Vegas convention and said she felt attacked. I was devastated because I thought I somehow truly offended her until she explained—whew!—politely with just the right humbling amount of condescension for me.

So, yes, even *you*, my audacious one, have an inner good girl—and if she's anything like mine, it's likely she can be harder to ghost than a regretful spring break social media post.

Like reprogramming ourselves away from so many unhealthy habits, we begin with tackling ghosts of a different kind: the ghosts of our childhood. Maybe you were fortunate enough to grow up in an enlightened and progressive environment where you were just loved for being you. And if so, *yay!* Let's be and raise women that feel accepted and amplified for their authentic selves. But maybe (like more of us) you grew up in more of a regular old environment where mom and dad did their best and meant well but WTF. Maybe one of the elements of your childhood that made its mark on your heart was the association between achievement and affection. Meaning the primary way you experienced big love from your mom or received positive attention from your dad was when you put points on the board. When you got the A. Or cleaned your room. Or did the backyard chores. Or free-babysat your younger siblings (again). Or "went with the flow" and didn't "rock the boat" even when things didn't go the way you had hoped or had been promised. So being the smart cookie that you are, you learned there was a value exchange, and the equation was simple: achievement and approval equal love and affection. And while there are certainly elements of that parenting strategy that have served you well in terms of your work ethic, there are also components that may have accidentally stuck around a little longer, like feelings of having to prove your worth, earn your emotional validation, or tend to other strange deep-seated layers that come with this evolved awareness of the understated ways your childhood continues to show up in your adulthood.

Perhaps, your inner good girl stems from the memories of negative reinforcement. Maybe you spilled something by accident or broke something on the wrong day; and maybe whoever was in charge of you not only exploded with anger but then ignored you outright. That person's extreme displeasure might have been enough to trigger you to clam up at any hint of discord. Being on the receiving end of a grudging silent treatment for making an innocent kid mistake in the wrong place at the wrong time might trigger a good-girl response that you still haven't managed to shake off.

Maybe you witnessed the most precarious of all: a double standard of what the women in your family were expected to do versus the men when it came to certain roles and responsibilities. Maybe the implied (but not always articulated) vibe was that the boys in the family "will be boys." (What does that mean? Well, apparently it meant that the dudes in your family were allowed to get away with stuff you weren't.) Maybe it was little things like curfews and cleanups or major things like having a strong opposing viewpoint actually taken seriously without being interrupted. Maybe you never even noticed it, but now that you're considering it, you might be wondering, where did this masculinity madness even come from?

Let's take a quick dip back into history to understand how this strange concept of the "good girl" came to be at a universal level, shall we? While there are a million reasons things "are the way they are," the OG reason for the myth of the good girl can be traced all the way back to the existence of historical inheritance systems in biblical times.

Most of us can agree objectively that in not all but many cases, money is power, yes? And while it's certainly far down the list of what should be most important in life after family, health, and an excellent dry shampoo, it is the currency that powers most of Maslow's hierarchy of needs elements of survival. Which kind of explains how we got here. If you're from a rural area, you may be familiar with the saying "The son gets the farm." Meaning the sons in the family are the focus, the priority, and automatically the recipients of wealth. They don't have to be "good boys" to earn it; they just have to possess a Y chromosome.

So because only male heirs were allowed to control property and because it wasn't until 1850 in the United States (in Oregon only!) that an unmarried woman was allowed to own property, centuries later men still enjoy (both visible and invisible) levels of patriarchal power built upon this ancient foundation. In other words, if you are a dude, you enjoy incredible life advantages and automatic privileges just for being a man. And as a feminist who *loves* men, I can tell you that some of my biggest male mentors and most successful champions totally agree that this patriarchal power thing is way real. And way old school. And way not cool.

And so this confusing, invisible, sexist virus has been allowed to infect our professional culture with alarming contagion. Maybe you're familiar with one of the social "name-swapping" experiments? Several have been done in the last decade, and the gist is this: You ask individuals to read about an employee named Jack who has a powerful working style and rate his leadership potential. Jack is rated favorably as "ambitious" and "efficient."

Then you ask another person to read the exact same scenario, except you swap out the name "Jack" for "Jane." How does the feedback change? Suddenly, you'll see the adjectives change, going, for example, from the positive "ambitious" to the negative "aggressive." Whereas Jack is a "go-getter," Jane is "pushy." Jack is "efficient," but Jane is "manipulative."

If you are one of my fellow corporate gals who have logged your fair share of boardroom hours at the highest echelons of the world's biggest companies, it's likely that you have your own first-person anecdotes supporting this bogus fiasco that's sadly still true. Even with diversity and inclusivity programs, even with sexual harassment training, even with affirmative action, even with all the Sheryls "leaning in" in the world, when it comes to corporate America (and to a lesser degree, small business and the gig economy), many of us still find ourselves existing at a professional intersection that looks like the elephant enclosure at the zoo—and smells the same. And that awful, dung-pocked intersection is at the corner of Respected but Not Liked Lane and Liked but Not Respected Road. When people think of a CEO, they still typically think of an old, white male with an immaculate suit and a steely gaze. (Even *with* Lauren Conrad's audaciously awesome moment on a radio show when she was asked an inappropriate question about her favorite position. To which she replied, "CEO."*) LC #FTW.

Look, it's no secret that oftentimes guys get paid more for the same work. A newly promoted guy is rarely queried on how he's going to manage his career *and* his family, but women promoted

---

* If you haven't seen this, give it a Google.

to the same position often are. As women in the public eye, we have our appearance judged before we even open our mouths to speak, and yet no one cares if a male leader looks hungover and wrinkled while wearing the same suit a month in a row.

The point of this whole tirade? A lot of this is super–messed up from way back when, and although we can't control the past, the promising news is that there are absolutely aspects of it that we *can* control when it comes to how we respond to this slowly improving reality in the present. Only *you*, not Instagram, your parents, your friends, or even a book like this, can intentionally and bravely decide how you want to operate within this reality to create the life you want to live. Only you can decide how to respond to these realities in an impactful way to shape or reshape your future.

In this chapter we're going to dissect how you can ghost your good-girl tendencies in your own life. And what you'll start to see is that every time you complete another successful ghosting, your audacity muscles will build. You'll watch as you'll begin equipping yourself with the strength needed to maximize the everyday opportunities to project your Big Deal Energy. Over time your BDE will compound into Massive Deal Energy that morphs into the extraordinary life that you and your journal have always fantasized about together.

And as a bonus? Remember that every time you have the BDE to show up audaciously, another woman is watching. Every time you have the guts to *do* the thing, *say* the thing, or *decide* the thing, you inspire others to have the audacity to green-light their own bold, big scary choice. And *that* is the type of courageous contagion we must ignite. That is the Big Deal movement women all over the world have been waiting for and working toward. Because together, we are ready for it. All of it.

But before we take on global feminine activation, let's start just a tad smaller, by ghosting our inner good girls once and for all.

GREETING YOUR GOOD GIRL

I'm 99.9 percent sure you know what ghosting is, but in case you don't, it's a term used to describe what happens when someone you are dating ends the relationship by cutting off all communication without explanation. Harsh? Yes. Necessary to shut down decades of patriarchal and familial programming? Also yes.

Before we get to how we can ghost that inner good girl, it's important to unpack precisely where these incoming messages will attempt to be delivered. Politely, of course. Your inner good girl typically shows up in three ways: permission asking, approval seeking, and perpetual people pleasing. Becoming hyperaware of those three typical triggers is the fastest way to silence your typical knee-jerk responses. So you've likely heard at least one of these terms casually tossed around on social media, but if you've been placing them all in the same bucket, it's a valuable undertaking to delineate the difference between each of these three good-girl grenades. We can't decisively defeat what we don't deliberately define.

Speaking of defining, let's just pause for a hot sec and ensure that we're crystal clear on the specific differences between the three. *Permission asking* paralyzes you from moving forward without a green light from some else. It renders you unable to authorize your *own* forward momentum.

We can't decisively defeat what we don't deliberately define.

Next, *approval seeking* is something that we all crave and do to a certain extent, but what happens when the approval of your choices from others unhealthily eclipses your approval of yourself?

And finally, *perpetual people pleasing*. The key here is "perpetual." Of course, we all want to make the ones we love happy—and that's obviously healthy, kind, loving, and so vital to nurturing our priceless relationships. But what we're talking about here is constant, pervasive people pleasing to the point where you've replaced your own happiness with that of others—where you've rebranded others' happiness as your own.

AX ASKING FOR PERMISSION

Let's start with the deadliest of the three good-girl grenades: asking for permission when permission really isn't needed. (To be clear, unless you are a dependent living at home with your parents or are looking to use someone's copyrighted material, phrases, or images, you do not need to ask permission to make a single decision in your life. Full stop.)

When did you first realize you *didn't* need to ask permission for everything you did? Maybe it was the first time someone told you that you didn't have to raise your hand to speak after years of being taught as a child that you're required to signal for permission to express yourself, that you were authorized to communicate independently as you saw fit?

For me, that moment was back when I was studying English at the University of Maryland. I was in a class of about 20 people studying the "screwed-up personal but brilliant professional life" of Ernest Hemingway. The professor was a proponent of a less formal, more casual, conversational-style learning experience, so she didn't require that we raise our hands. I remember having that mortified fast-heartbeat feeling when she reminded me, as I raised my hand yet again, that if I had something to contribute, I should green-light myself to do so. Was I embarrassed that I was having trouble reprogramming my childhood software? Mortified that she had to grant me permission to not request permission? Flustered that my formality was shamefully nonfeminist? Correct answer: *D:* all of the above!

Fast-forward to grown-up life. Obviously, you're no longer physically raising your hand to speak,* but have you ever considered how it might be showing up for you in other, less obvious ways? Whether the "teacher" asking for your good-girl permission slip is an individual or an institution in your life, school has been out for a *lonnnng* time now, my friend.

---

* I hope not. If you are, leave that cult immediately.

Maybe for you, your permission seeking is still chasing you around in your current corporate environment or with certain "legacy industry" client interactions. One day, my friend Sam shared with me that she found herself shrinking away from speaking up in meetings. She never had a problem sharing her ideas and expressing her two cents until one particularly distressing meeting. At that particular meeting, Sam had articulately (maybe too articulately?) expressed a dissenting opinion in response to an assertive male colleague. In front of the full conference room of peers, she was shut down by the most senior manager—who was a male friend of that colleague. Sam was so astonished and dismayed by the way the manager dismissed her fair counterargument that she kept a low profile in meetings going forward. She was anxious and distressed that she would be slapped with the modern-day office version of the scarlet letter A: "aggressive."

The experience was one of those "can't stop replaying it for weeks afterward" moments. One that she played like a mental boomerang to the point that Sam inadvertently went to the equally detrimental extreme of being *too* passive. She didn't realize she began waiting to give her opinion only if someone directly asked her for it. Which, as you can probably already guess because maybe you've experienced this conundrum, is the classic catch-22. You know that enticing people to want to hear more of what we think only begins when they've heard a few other brilliant insights they're impressed with first, right? So as you might imagine, passively waiting around for someone to "call on her" school style was not exactly what you might call a winning strategy.

Over time, Sam's contributing value naturally came into question, which made her feel even more frustrated, steamrollered, and misunderstood. She felt alienated and unliked. Lonely, sad, and desperate, she assumed she was probably just going to get fired. She felt like an emotional Goldilocks: always too hot or too cold. And in that moment, she realized three things: (1) A mythical "just right" temperature did not exist for her. (2) It shouldn't be up to her to figure out how to find and maintain the perfect temperature in the room to keep everyone else comfortable. And (3) if she kept waiting around for someone at this stupid office to greenlight her to show up and speak up, she would implode. Or Jerry-Maguire out dramatically. Or both.

So she adjusted her own thermostat. She set it to "Screw it. I'm over this place; they can fire me if they want" degrees Celsius. Walking into a meeting later, she started to weigh in for the first time in months. Her listeners were nodding their heads in response when suddenly that same male colleague tried to interrupt her. She thought about one of the other women in the office who always fought to be heard, borrowed her bravery (more on this in Chapter 7), and just kept right on talking. She pretended she didn't even hear or see this guy. It was super-awkward as they both simultaneously kept talking for what seemed like ages (but was in reality about four seconds) until he backed down. He was miffed, astounded, and shocked.

What happened next? The entire conference room looked at him like *he* was the rude one, which of course he was. After the meeting and thoroughly fed up, she took a deep breath, walked up to him, looked him square in the eye, and calmly said, "Do . . . not . . . interrupt me . . . during a meeting . . . ever again. Got it?" Wide-eyed and aghast, he nodded. And he kept his word.

Four audacious seconds were the difference between Sam giving up or leveling up. Four seconds of holding her ground triggered the momentum to reignite her reputation and position both on her team and within the broader organization. At first, her coworkers and bosses didn't know what to do with this new "sassy" Sam. But slowly, one day, one decision, one encounter at a time, she started to find her internal champions and allies. She found her success stride. Most importantly, she found *her* "just right" temperature.

Like Sam, only *you* can authorize your own permission slip. Only *you* can crank up the volume on that microphone. Only *you* can call on yourself to step into your Big Deal Energy and say *enough is enough*.

Only you can call on yourself to step into your Big Deal Energy and say enough is enough.

#BIGDEALBOOK

So which will you choose? Will you give up, or will you level up? Are you encouraging *yourself* to level up your impact, your presence, your asks, your brand, your footprint, your network, your goals, your *dreams*?

Are you granting yourself permission to overcome and strategically deter interruptions? Especially the ones from dudes?

Especially the ones from dudes who currently make more money than you do? Especially the ones from dudes who make more money than you partially because the manager is their golf buddy?

Are you trashing permission-seeking phrases like "Sorry," "Just an idea," or "I could be totally wrong, but . . ."?

Are you green-lighting your own powerful voice, no matter which table—boardroom or dining room or both—that you're seated around?

Are you adjusting your own audacity thermostat and setting it to a temperature that is more effective for what you're chasing down? Is there something in front of you right now that could use a little turn of the audacity dial? A little dose of your BDE? Will you turn it? It's my hope that your answer is yes, because your life is too precious to spend it shivering in the cold.

QUIT YOUR APPROVAL HABIT

Is there anything that feels better than someone agreeing with your idea like you are Einstein reincarnated? Of course not. It feels *so* fantastic to be retweeted whether online or offline, personally or professionally. *And yet*—the second good-girl grenade that needs to be dismantled, like, *yesterday*, is addiction to *his* or *her* approval. Whose approval do you know that you shouldn't crave but you just "can't help yourself"? Does your approval Achilles' heel reveal itself in fishing for compliments from your partner? Craving recognition from your boss? Being thirsty for likes on the internet?

No matter your case, dropping this habit of approval seeking so you can feel good about yourself—or what you believe in—*without* that external thumbs-up is crucial. Why? Because if you depend on others for approval, you're choosing a scary fast track to accelerating anxiety, developing depression, or sabotaging your self-esteem. Now if that sounds a little dramatic, and you're thinking, *WHOA, Erin, I'm not that bad*, let me ask you this: are you sure? Have you ever opened one of your social apps and been swallowed up by a tsunami of digital approval?

"You're so gorgeous!"

"You look amazing!"

Fire emoji fire emoji fire emoji

"Yesss, Queen"

"Dang, girl!"

Cue the dopamine dance party! With each comment, your ego sinks deeper into that bubble bath of digital bliss. Light that candle, pour the champagne, and let the narcissism nightingale sing sweet songs of selfie success. So what's so dangerous about that? Well technically nothing . . . *if* it stops there.

But what about when it doesn't? Oh, you liked that photo, random girl from high school? Wait until you see *this one*! Or even better, *this one*! Wait, there's more! Ding, ding, ding, dopamine hit! The hits keep coming, and the addict stays addicted. . . .

Until one photo doesn't get as many likes, and you find yourself deleting it. On the next caption you spend an embarrassing amount of time carefully crafting, obsessing over the cleverest wording you can think of. That one didn't do as well? Maybe you reshoot, refilter, recaption, repost, and finally get your fix as you experience endorphin hit after endorphin hit when the approvals stack up.

The next time, maybe you're on the fence about a post. Cue the origin of "felt cute, might delete later." What does that mean? *I like myself right now, but if you don't, I'll just delete it (along with a little piece of my #selfrespect)*. You're essentially approving your decision to let everyone else's approval potentially override your own later. No. *Nope*. Would you give any physical person in your offline life that much control over your self-esteem? Then why are you doing it now in your personal *or* professional life?

OK, I know, I know. The reality of living in today's hybrid offline-online reality means that every time you share anything, you are essentially seeking approval. None of us posts something that we want people to disapprove of, and none of us speaks up at work to get shot down. Obviously.

Now, is it your fault that social media and iPhones were designed intentionally to mimic casino slot machines and scientifically hook our brains to be obsessed with tapping the "pull down and refresh" technology for another hit? No, of course not. If you've watched *The Social Dilemma* on Netflix, you know we are all caught in a terrifyingly complex web of being watched, hooked, and manipulated like a SoCal *Succession*-style billionaire whose kids are burning though their trust funds. And loving to receive love online can be relatively harmless *until* this same "please love me" mentality crosses over into approval seeking in other aspects of our "real," or offline, life—relationships, business ventures, or even failures! If your fear of failure often stems from your fear of what others will think of you, is it any wonder you'll continue to crave the approval that accompanies success?

If you choose to stay stuck in a constant approval-seeking endless loop with the world weighing in on everything from your choices and opinions to your business ideas and weekend outfits, guess whose fault that is? It's not Mark Zuckerberg's algorithm's fault. It's not your mom's either. It. Is. *Yours.*

I know that feels harsh, because it *isn't* your fault that 24/7 social media has dumped digital fuel onto our flames of desire for approval. It *isn't* your fault that social reprogramming is infecting every facet of our lives. But it is your fault if you choose to throw water on that mogwai. You are the only one who can seize the opportunity to take back control and make stronger, more empowering choices. You are the only one who can optimize your mentality so you can avoid getting burned.

You cannot live a life that is fully *real* and fully *yours and* have it be what the internet says it should be. Or what your older sister, best friend from high school, well-meaning boss, or over-the-line client thinks. It's challenging but not impossible to break this "Is this OK?" habit. You just have to be audacious AF. Let's consider a few strategies to move away from too much time sad-scrolling. Let's stop looking at everyone else's paper so we can start freeing more time and space and energy for you to grace the world with your particular brand of BDE. Let's slay this limiting habit by you asking yourself some complex queries.

Can you determine *why* you feel that you need this person's (or this network's) approval? And when your first answer comes to mind, I want you to ask *why* again. And again. And again.

Like a Simon Sinek–crazed toddler, I want you to keep poking holes until you peel your onion layers back to surface your real, ultimate reason. Go beyond the bland response of "It just feels good," because duh. Dig deeper. Why *else* are you wanting this so badly? This is undoubtedly a complex question with some truly messy answers. Why do you need others to love what you're doing for you to love it? Whether it's a lifestyle, a relationship, or another big choice, can you ask yourself why you need this so much that you can't move forward comfortably without the person's "*Yay, you!*"?

It's natural for us to want the people we love to love our decisions. You can want that, and wish for that, but you don't *need it*. Now, I need you to really hear me on this one. There are two categories of relationships in your life right now: *your people* and everyone else. *Your people*—the ones who really know you and still love you—will only ever truly approve of one practice: *you being authentically, honestly, radically you*. And everyone else? Bless and block.

Your people—the ones who really know you and still love you—will only ever truly approve of one practice: you being authentically, honestly, radically you.

If you truly want to cross over from where you are to the dimension you're destined to exist within, you must find the faith to unfriend unsolicited outside approval. Can you find a way in your heart to finally *know* that you really, *really* do not need it? And if you still feel like you do need it? Or that the "approver" needs you to need it? Tragically but truthfully, it's time to migrate that person from the category of "your people." Maybe that person *was* part of your people, but because of life, circumstances, change, and time, that person has slipped from that special seat. And that totally sucks as much a Brazilian wax given by a timid little old lady. It's painful and arduous, and it's hell while it's happening; but when it's finished, you will strut away feeling lighter, more confident, and ready for anything life throws your way.

Can you practice *rejoicing* in rejection? I know, *rejoice* sounds over-the-top extra when we're talking about leaving people behind who once meant so much to you, but we both know it needs to happen so you can achieve those Big Deal dreams.

So how can you begin to rejoice in *your* relationship with rejection? Let's start by identifying the most self-assured person you know. Someone who seems blatantly bulletproof. Someone who doesn't take things too seriously when they don't work out or if they make a spectacle of themselves. What does this marvelous marauder do for work? I'm willing to bet that during at least one chapter of their lives, they worked in *some* type of sales role. Whether they were a formal professional corporate salesperson, a bartender, or the person that gets everyone to donate to charity, the person you've identified oozes sexy unstoppable BDE because they've put in the rejection reps. Their internal bounce-back biceps are Rambo level from use and abuse. Like their morning spin class or nighttime pushups, they showed up and sweated out the snubs on a daily no-matter-what basis. And that has made them *unstoppable* when it comes to chasing down the opportunities they know they were born to unlock.

Let me ask you this: have you ever been hung up on? I mean straight up someone decided that he or she could not stand being electrically linked to you for another second, so the person just killed the connection with a punched button to the face? If not, I highly recommend you manage to be "hung up on." Why? Well, let's just say that the first year of my "real-world job" as a 100 percent commission-only sales rep, I was yelled at or hung up on at least 20 times a day. If there are about 250 working days in a year, that's 5,000 rejections at the tender, insecure age of 22. And I would *not* trade that experience for the world! Because building up that resilience and grit—however you can—is the only way to not let the fact that some guy didn't call you back send you into a tailspin. Or the fact that that one client rejected your proposal, so now you're scared to play it big when it comes to closing the next one.

Getting straight up rejected is, IMHO, the most efficient way for you to know how to quickly get back up when you didn't get the gig, the sale, the job, or the invite. It's the only way to cultivate the courage to raise capital from alpha dudes for a tampon business—and then ultimately "fail" at that. It's the only way to reinvent again by deciding who you and your talents are truly for. It's the only way to ride out a global pandemic where you had to blow up and start over even though you had *just* been acquiring the traction you'd been scraping by for. The definition of insanity might be doing the same thing over and over and expecting a different result, but the definition of audacity is doing the same thing over and over again and not *caring* if anyone thinks you're insane. That's how you can inoculate yourself against your inner good girl regaining any kind of footing within your feelings.

So here's my action ask: Is there some way you might be able to intentionally put yourself in a situation or two to raise your rejection risk tolerance? If you aren't in sales, how might you get some kind of sales experience? Even if it's trying to sell someone you work with on a new idea? If you are in sales, how can you ask for more money? Go for a bigger client? Color outside the corporate lines? Show up in a way that is maybe so authentic, so aggressive, so "not how we do things," that maybe it's a tad shocking? And if all this sounds *wayyy* absurd to you, fair enough; let's dial it back to show up in a basic way. I dare you to post something on social media, and if it doesn't rain likes and crush with fire-emoji-laced comments, just leave it up. Don't delete it. Even though you don't "feel cute." The audacity activator here is for you to *not* think of it again. Who cares? Remember, people are looking at their own profiles more than yours anyway! What if you went for a gig, a job, or a promotion that you're pretty sure is out of your league? Or for a new hobby that you're pretty sure you would initially really suck at? Or ask out the person you think is "too good," "too hot," "too [*insert BS narrative here*]" for you?

When you start rolling the dice in more "rejection likely" scenarios, you'll start to reframe rejection as a fabulous friend. A friend who is sharing invaluable intel for how you might modify, improve, or show up bigger, stronger, and more courageously the next time. And when you do, I swear on my sales success scars you *will* see a change. You'll feel it. You'll know it in your beautifully bodacious bones. You'll see that the next time your boss or team leader has tons of changes, annoying suggestions, or "constructive feedback" to offer, instead of feeling that familiar wet blanket of despair or frustration, you'll take it with positivity and maybe even a scandalous sprinkle of motivation. Over time, you'll notice yourself processing all feedback differently. You'll organically take it with a grain (or a gallon) of salt, as opposed to the gospel it used to be. If you actually start to intentionally put yourself smack-dab in the middle of Rejection Road, the next time you don't get the invite to something or make the cut for a team or project, you *will* shrug it off faster, and you'll find that you've wasted zero time moving on to the next opportunity, the one that's a much better fit for you anyway.

Can you challenge yourself to be aware of those sneaky everyday opportunities to raise your rejection risk tolerance? You might have noticed there are some subtle, more passive-aggressive phrases disguised as "joking," that not only can cause major damage, but potentially might put you in the danger zone of death by a thousand cuts. How do you know if you're teetering on the edge of such devastating social ditches? Look for statements like, "You're just *a lot* sometimes." Or maybe "Could you *tone* it down?" Besides these being screaming indicators that the people saying them are *not* your people, these are also chances for you to ask them to explain why they feel like that. "Could you tell me why you think that?" and "Can you give me a specific example?" are ways to invite rejection in voluntarily, so you can take back control of your emotions, and possibly glean some invaluable insights to improve. Or, on the other hand, you'll create clarity around who these people *really* are, let their comments roll off like rain, and then vote them off your island! And replace them with people who *do* think you rock. Because you do. Because you and I both know that you're what? Because you are . . . *say it* . . . *kind of a Big Deal.*

The coolest part about getting better at real, legit rejection is that your life will improve on *all* the levels. Becoming a rejection rock star truly is a fast track to the freedom you know you're capable of feeling. Of course, there are endless ways to learn, grow, improve, and succeed. Of course, there are endless rejection responses from endless types of people, not because of what you have said, done, or decided, but because different strokes are simply for different folks. Rejection is *literally* just part of the process. It's an essential part of evolving from kind of a Big Deal to a fully Big Damn Deal. You have what it takes to become better at staying level-headed whether you get a "*Yay, you!*" or an "Oh no, not *you.*" or any reaction in between. Rejection rock stars are just better at rewriting life lyrics from a "no" to a "not yet" or "not a fit."

PAUSE YOUR PEOPLE PLEASING

At this point, you might be wondering whether you're just a super-nice gal in a healthy, kind human way or in a perpetual people pleaser way who is draining her emotional (and home wine supply) reservoir. Your self-diagnosis begins with asking yourself this: When you're trying to help others get what they want and what they need, does it ever get to a point where your own health starts to suffer? And I don't mean just being tired after staying up with a friend hyperanalyzing breakup texts into the wee hours. That's called being a bestie. I'm talking about long-term, chronic health issues triggered by being too nice, for too long, to too many people, without replenishment of your own reserves. Let's identify some of our own audacity-assaulting suspects so we can effectively eliminate them, like, yesterday.

YOU *DESPISE* SAYING NO

Sure, we've all abhorred declining someone or something, feeling the guilties (mini guilty vibes) that pop up when you refuse a small ask on a packed day. No, I'm talking about being someone who *despises* saying no.

I fall into this category as a recovering people pleaser, particularly when it comes to declining most invitations, avoiding overcommitting, and just generally managing boundaries between myself and those around me. If you've ever found you agreed to multiple events the same day or night, I hate to tell you this, but you, like me, might struggle with being a PPP (perpetual people pleaser).

If you've overcommitted to the point where you're saying "sorry" for letting someone down one too many times, you are a PPP. If you find yourself wincing or gritting your teeth as someone makes an ask that you know you cannot or *do not want* to do, but you can feel this alternate version of you smiling and nodding your head as your inner GPS lady is saying *nooooo . . . signal lost!*, you are a PPP. If the drug campaign from the eighties of "Just Say No" feels unrealistic for you, you're not alone! It's because *no* is the word of rejection. And just like being rejected doesn't feel good, neither does being the rejecter! And obviously as the kind human that you are, you don't want to spread sad darkness; you want to be an amplifier of the light! You want to be the glitter, the rainbows, and the sparkle of every room you float into, not the "buzzkill bearing bad news."

Have you ever watched someone decline something so gracefully and just thought, "*Wow*. I wish I could do that!" Well, that's my friend Kara. She is the *master* of saying no with elegance and the queen of setting (and defending) highly healthy boundaries. I'll never forget watching her in action when we worked together at an early "connection platform" (which was basically an early LinkedIn competitor; obviously, LinkedIn won). Kara is someone who is *extremely* charitable (strategically so) with her time. She volunteers at a home for the elderly and helps raise funds for inner-city schools. She shows up at your life milestone soiree with cards, gifts, and a big "Yay, you!" smile. She is the consummate benevolent bestie to so many women who are each beyond honored to call her a compadre.

But *because* of this, she is personally and professionally *constantly* in higher demand than Grubhub orders during a pandemic. And we all know how it feels to be hungry and see that "order canceled" notification. So, over the years, she has developed the most magical methods for turning people down without turning them off. She delivers yes's antonym so masterfully that the people she is keeping at bay not only aren't insulted or upset; they're almost apologetic that they've overstepped *their* bounds. They act regretful to have imposed on *her*. It's seriously an art form.

The first thing Kara taught me is when you find yourself in a situation where you need to say no but you feel like you can't (i.e., a boss is asking something of you that is above and beyond your job description, or a friend is asking for a romantic introduction to one of your high-profile LinkedIn contacts), the key to a successful decline is to never actually *use*, *utter*, or *type* the word *no*. Remember, being audacious is not about going through life torching villages and hearts and happiness like a narcissistic asshole. In Kara's case, in one of her opening tactics, not only does she not utter the word *no*; she miraculously doesn't say anything at all. I have watched her in a million situations where someone—a work colleague, a PTA mom, or a friend—will request something she simply physically does not have the bandwidth to deliver on. Let's say there just isn't room in her calendar, whether it's drawing up someone else's contract or baking cupcakes for someone else's fund-raiser. Here's what she does. (And I'm not suggesting you mimic this, as it's very odd. I'm just giving you a peek behind the scenes of a master decliner. Do with this transparency what you will.) She will look at the person, bite her lip or frown, and then just stare off at some point in the distance. And she says nothing. Nothing! Awkward? Yes. This silence has its own sweat! And then she just *waits*.

And guess what happens? Every time, the requester breaks the silence first, but now this person has moved from a position of being in authority to being a little off-balance, because he or she is totally bewildered and rattled. So the person asks again as if Kara didn't hear, or he or she repeats the question, and Kara responds with some version of one of the following:

- "I would love to help you however I realistically can. I'm just going to need some more information/details to make sure." And she then proceeds to ask for *so* much information about time, place, people, goals, deliverables, logistics, budgets, dress code, allergy-gluten-dairy-free catering, and side perks for herself, her friends, and her dog that oftentimes the person just backs off and says, "Ah! I'm so sorry. I guess I need to find out more details for you. Can I circle back with you?"

- "I would love to help you however I realistically can. It's just that right now I have a full plate with [*xyz*], but might a future date work, like [*vague date*]? Would that work for you?" Typically, this date is way too late, and when the person tells her that, she doesn't say sorry; she just says "Ahhh, darn! Maybe next time!"

- "Possibly! I have this project, and this deadline, and this commitment, and [*xyz*], but I could *try* and find some time. I don't know when, of course, but . . ." She literally just rattles off the most insanely detailed schedule to the point that the person apologizes to *her* for having imposed. It's incredible.

- "Ugh, I wish I could. [*Give no excuse.*] Can I think about a better fit to help you with this and circle back with you?" Again, the person is grateful for the offer to be connected with someone better suited. (Which, of course, you then have to do.)

Kara has taught me *sooooo* many ways to say no to ghost her inner people-pleasing good girl without passing on the bad vibes of making someone you care about suffer the sting of rejection. That's one end of the audacity spectrum. On the other end of the spectrum is a different brand of BDE keeping her inner PPP at bay. This tactic can be used when people ask you to do something that you know you can't or don't want to do: You pause (the long pause is *key*), sigh, and just say, "There is absolutely no possible way that is realistically possible for me at all." And then you look at them with a bit of diva sass, resisting the urge to break the silence (we don't always have to fill the silence!), and 9 times out of 10, they will be so shocked by how dramatically direct you were, they will burst out laughing in disbelief. And then you just shrug your shoulders with a "sorry not sorry sister" look on your face. Case clearly closed. BDE FTW.

See, deep down, it's likely that you aren't actually afraid of saying no. You're certainly not quaking in your UGGs from uttering that little itty-bitty word itself. What makes all of us sweat a skosh is the potentially negative response that could be attached to you when you do. Using one of Kara's brilliant strategic language choices, you can nip that no in the bud and start creating the *space*, *time*, and *energy* that you know you need to prioritize your needs. You can't focus on tackling what's most meaningful to you and what's essential for today when you simply don't have the actual room in your mind, your heart, or your calendar to do so properly.

When it comes to boundary setting, again, Kara is the no-grudge guru. I've seen her tell her bosses, point-blank, that their requests are not going to work for her. In a very upbeat, positive way, she sets boundaries by staying focused on what's in it for *them*, should they agree to respect her desire to work from home, keep certain hours, not be able to respond immediately, work with certain people, or do things with a certain methodology. Persuasion is personal, right? Her power phrase for disarming even the most curmudgeonly of commanders: "Putting myself in your shoes, it seems like you're looking to . . . [*state the goal people are trying to accomplish*]." Rock the presentation, crush the numbers, produce the event successfully, surpass the competitor, implement the new initiative—*whatever it is they want or need*. (Pro tip: it's usually to ensure *their* boss knows how fabulous *they* are doing and up and up the chain. Remembering that your boss has a boss is the fastest way to gain clarity on what people truly care about.)

Kara waits until she gets the tentative head nod. (The simple yet sacred step to getting people to agree to anything you're requesting after that.) She continues, "So knowing how I work best, to ensure we are set up for maximum success when it comes to [*repeat the goal*], I'm going to need to [*set boundary*]."

When you do this, you are positioning your needs being met or respected as a critical factor to ensure *their* needs are ultimately met, too. Boom, boundary set. Relationship intact. You win! Forget your inner good girl; that's just called being good. Full stop.

RELEASE THE RESENTMENT

Carrie Fisher, aka Princess Leia,* once said that being resentful is like drinking poison and waiting for the other person to die. If you're finding yourself being angry without a reason when it comes to the other people in your life, it's likely because maybe you have been secretly sipping from the chalice of suppressed issues for far too long. And what your inner GPS lady is repeating to you like a madwoman is this: "rerouting, rerouting, rerouting." Whose destination are you plugging in? Yours? Or someone else's? When you're neglecting where you're trying to go in favor of riding shotgun on too many other people's road trips, eventually you run out of gas. You're running on fumes and you stutter to a stop, and now you're in the middle of the desert and your phone is dead and you don't have any water. Why did you use up *all* your gas, your cell phone battery, and your water on someone else *again*?

One of my very oldest friends is so dear to me and breaks my heart because she finds herself in this exact situation time and time again. And while she is so fun, and so generous and extremely successful, deep down (which comes out now and then like a volcano of rage) she is also *really* damn angry. Why? Well, this is the situation: Both of her parents are super-achieving lawyers, and so naturally her whole life, she was groomed to be a lawyer. We're talking childhood Christmas photo where she is wearing a onesie from her parents' law school alma mater.

---

* It's impossible that you've never seen *Star Wars*. But if you haven't, this footnote is officially assigning it to you as homework.

So her path was set. It was decided. Prechosen, like she was Harry Potter.

And like a good daughter, who loves her parents and doesn't want to disappoint them, she followed the path they set out for her. One time, she remembers timidly sharing with her parents that she was thinking about applying to culinary school, since she *loves* to cook. Her parents about had a heart attack and chastised her into shelving that dream for a *never* day. And so she did. Fast-forward to today, and she's a damn good lawyer, partly because she's so pissed off all the time. But, at the end of the day, she is ultimately *choosing* good-girl status over a good-life one. Her parents may be thrilled and proud, but when we have those "How are you *really* feeling?" wine night debriefs, she admits that her life is not what she thought it would be. That she's "fine" but not necessarily thrilled with how her life has turned out so far. Is that gold star perfect-daughter status really worth the price of admission for her when she'd rather be whipping up crème brûlée?

Or maybe you're like another friend of mine who drives herself *insane* obsessing over everyone else's wins. Someone else's promotion, closed deal, or award feels like a direct rejection of her. Every time someone else gets the "What a brilliant idea!" that she doesn't, she gets down on herself. Why? Because she craves the good-girl accolade like a marathon runner craves water. She was one of these people who consistently outperformed her peers in school and was used to being at the top of her class. But like many academics, a prowess for memorization and organization doesn't always translate to guaranteed professional success. If you know someone like this, or maybe this is hitting a little too close to home for you, you know this is a total lose-lose situation. With every moment she spends internalizing that resentment toward her coworkers' success, she is keeping herself even more stuck and even further from capturing it for herself. Because holding on to those scarcity mentality emotions are pure and total emotional toxicity. And there is no negotiating with toxicity terrorists. There is only cutting them off, turning your back, and digging deep to find a way to slap yourself with your own sparkly sticker. Or even better, get the heck over it, because stickers are for small children, not Big Deal baddies like yourself who know there is an infinite abundance of success to go around for all of us. Right? *Right?* Release your resentment. Run away from it. Far and fast. Because you have too much to do, be, and see to waste your precious special moments on this earth trapped inside your parents' or society's or whoever else's agenda you may or may not consciously *realize* you're following. Don't be good at being a good girl. Be great at being a gritty one.

YOU'RE NOT THE FAV. SO WHAT?

Do you have a friend who is legit obsessed with being the favorite in her family? Or in her friend group? She's tricky to spot because, remember, being the good girl makes everyone else super-stoked. She delivers the copious compliments. She sends the lovely hand-written cards, including a thank you note for your thank you note. She shows up to everything no matter how tired, busy, stressed, or sad she actually is. If her relationship deposits were real currency, she'd have a loaded bank balance account. That's totally one of my dear neighbor-friends here in California. Now you're probably thinking, "Um, can I be friends with this person? She sounds like the perfect bestie!" And therein lies the problem. It's fine if your friend is doing all those things because she authentically loves to and genuinely wants to. But where it becomes an audacity smotherer is when that same friend finds that others have gone beyond appreciation to inadvertently taking advantage of her emotional generosity.

Have you ever been friends with someone you let make more withdrawals from than deposits into your friendship bank in the name of "being a good person"? This same gal is usually the one who lets the guys she dates set the agenda without making it clear what's actually truly important to her. (Through gritted teeth and a plastered tight smile: *I don't care if we don't get engaged, really! I just love us as we are.* If this is true, yay for you. But Disney princess programming is hard to shake, so if you don't mean it, don't say it!) If you've ever found yourself overcommitting to "helping out" your coworkers to the point that you are loaded down with projects that are far beyond your job description, you are likely venturing dangerously close to deadly levels of people pleasing.

Important disclaimer here: yes, in the early days of your career, showing up, saying yes, going the extra mile to differentiate yourself and carve out your place is smart and highly recommended. What I'm talking about here is different though. It's that slippery slope, that accidental place where those behaviors persist for a decade or more after you've earned your stripes and proved yourself.

Back to my neighborhood bud. This quest for winning the golden child award even extends into her romantic life, where she is clearly *perfectly happy* with being single. She's very independent and very particular and actually *thrives* on living alone. She's a social butterfly who loves being the life of the party with the freedom to buzz around from one convo to the next. If she truly wanted to settle down with someone by now, she would have! She's smart, sexy, successful . . . and she's actually quite fulfilled and happy as a free and independent party of one.

The problem? Her being single deeply disappoints her family members, and they aren't afraid to communicate it. "Where are the cousins? The grandkids?" And being that she is super-close to said family members, in an effort to please them and cling to her fast-fading good-girl status, she keeps at that dating game and the apps even though it's been clear for decades that she is *much* happier and healthier and more content being solo. I know, right? How dare she? A woman who is fulfilled without committing to the one forever lifelong romantic partner? The scandal of it!

As you can imagine, ignoring her inner GPS on her relationship routine does nothing but block her BDE. One time, I was sharing with her about how I planned on setting boundaries with someone else, and her response was passive-aggressive: "Oh why am I surprised? Of course, you'll just tell them what *you* want to have happen!" Her resentment and jealousy toward me were palpable. Why would my talking about how I'm going to handle something in my life have anything to do with her or make her angry? Because once again, big actions trigger big reactions. When people come at you like that, it's a textbook reflection of how your Big Deal decision is making them feel about their own challenges. And every time she witnessed my invisible middle finger at the "should life" in favor of the "good one," it reminded her that she wasn't having the gusto to do the same in her own sticky scenarios. That she was staying stuck within these invisible, self-imposed good-girl boundaries no matter how miserable they were making her. That the scenarios in her life that drained her the most stemmed from ultimately prioritizing the preferences of her family above her own to a physically unhealthy degree. It forced her to reexamine her trusty old familiar narrative of blame in a way that made her seriously squirm. It reminded her that the only person she had to blame for her emotional restlessness was not her family, but herself. It reminded her that she *did* have a choice, and the choice she was making was to preserve her inner good girl at the expense of her inner GPS lady. Good girl, 1; inner GPS lady, 0. And that is a score in the game of life that if you've played, and most of us have, you know it typically ends stuck in one sad locker room.

Have you ever had that sort of a reaction to people who were just sharing what they were doing and wondered why you were acting like such a psycho? I know I have! Unexplainable anger toward others for no practical reason is like being emotionally hangry. It's your body's way of letting you know your soul's blood sugar is low and you're in desperate need of emotional glucose.

If you find yourself being like my friend, can you have the emotional maturity to ask yourself *why*? Can you really dig deep to identify exactly who you are so desperate to make happy and if it's truly worth it?

How can you be more intentional about recognizing when you're not being totally honest with yourself or when you're buying your own excuses for good-girl goof-ups? How can you focus less on being the "good daughter," the "good sister," or the "good friend" and more on being good to *yourself*? By being audacious. And this doesn't mean you have to stop caring about what anyone thinks of you, but you do have to care *more* about what *you* think of you.

JOIN THE GLOBAL GOOD-GIRL GHOSTING SOCIETY

If you just read that heading and pictured a Carmen Sandiego–like squad of kick-butt superlady spies, you aren't far off from the theme of this section. If you've ever gotten goose bumps reading about the brave women throughout history who risked their lives for equality, you know that we are so beyond fortunate to stand on the sister shoulders of giants. We are *so lucky* to have followed the suffragettes and the women's movement and so energized as we experience the modern-day #MeToo tidal wave. Their courage, strength, and sheer audacity have made *huge* leaps in the last hundred years for women's equality. We have opportunities today that our own mothers couldn't even have imagined, thanks to them.

Yes, in 2020, about half of women were the primary bread-winners in their household and/or were outearning their husbands. *Yes*, we have it much, *much* better than many women in all kinds of places around the world who survive and fight against incomprehensible rights violations on a daily basis. All over the world, there are chill-inducing stories of feminist heroes of all ages, backgrounds, and challenges, and all these women have one thing in common—they *refuse* to go quietly.

And no matter where you are in the world as you are reading this, no matter what type of family, culture, or space you find yourself in at the moment, you have a responsibility to yourself, your current or future children, and your current or future grandchildren to fight for a world where good girls are brave girls. Authentic ones. Ones who speak out, disrupt, and invent. It's up to us to create a future where boldness is applauded and respected, not muzzled and judged. And it starts with you, and it starts with me, and it starts with all of us tackling the smallest everyday scenarios everywhere from boardrooms to bedrooms where our inner good girls are no longer welcome. And every time you have the audacity to do just that in your own life, *you* are contributing to hell-yes herd immunity. You are being the light that the next generations of women watching you—and they are watching—need to be able to disrupt the status quo, pick up that torch, and shine brightness into even the darkest moments.

✳ BIG DEAL DIARY ✳

Time to do a little good-girl ghostbusting. As you read through the following questions, listen to yourself for the first answers that come to mind. Write your answers freely, without judging:

✳ Why do I want their approval? Why are you *really* looking for validation in the first place? This is the first step to gaining control of how addicted you might be to it.

- Does your answer have to do with childhood?

- Or maybe more recent events?

- Does this behavior manifest more in your personal or your professional life?

- If this happens in one arena, but not the other, examine what triggers it where it does occur.

- How will you commit to stop permission seeking?

- How will you commit to stop approval seeking?

- How will you commit to stop PPP: perpetual people pleasing?

✳ What do you need to ghost?

- What is one behavior you recognized in yourself from this chapter?

- Will you commit to eliminating it from your life?

- Will you agree to not work with it, or work around it, but completely leave it behind?

- If so, fill in the blank here: One good-girl behavior I commit to ghosting is

  _____.

- And the next time I find myself in this scenario, instead, I'm going to

  _____.

✸ Just say no:

- When you find yourself obsessing about a social media caption for too long or shying away from making a decision that is in alignment with your core values but that will displease someone you care about, can you *just say no* to making what someone else thinks of your decisions something for you to worry about or obsess over?

- What kinds of healthier social media behaviors can you let go of? Or optimize? Or start? As Eleanor Roosevelt said, "What other people think of me is none of my business."

- If your issue is in the professional realm, how can you elevate your focus above caring about what others think of your business or work choices?

✳ Ground rules:

🌀 What are your boundaries for how others may interact with you?

🌀 How do you enforce those?

🌀 If people stand you up once, they don't get a second chance. If people interrupt you, just keep talking. If people show you their true colors, believe them. This is your world: only you can decide how you permit people to be in your orbit.

🌀 Are you surrounding yourself with "your people"? If not, why not?

🌀 And what action might you take to spend more time with people who love you and get you *without* you having to work excessively over-the-top hard for it?

#BIGDEALBOOK

CHAPTER 4

BECOME A
BAD LISTENER

The Greek slave turned Stoic philosopher Epictetus said, "We were given two ears and one mouth so we can listen twice as much as we speak." And while I'm genuinely a huge fan of many Stoic principles (and all things Greek really—islands, salads, those gods and goddesses), I must respectfully and resolutely disagree with this quote. I know that sounds certifiably insane, but let me explain. (Yes, I'm asking you to please listen to me about listening less.) Yes, the world's greatest salespeople are the best listeners. Yes, listening actively to your client's needs, your team's challenges, your partner's emotions, your child's concerns, and your friend's problems are critically important to discover where the pain lies so that you can help soothe it. Yes, if you're a chiseled, marble-sculpture white

man in a toga—or a white male CEO in an expensive suit—
this philosophy is as solid as the statue himself. But here's the
truth: as twenty-first-century female leaders, entrepreneurs, creatives, and professionals operating in still male-dominated corporate industries and our still pretty patriarchal culture, if we
follow the advice to listen twice as much as we speak, we risk
never getting a word in. We risk not having the opportunity to
be heard. We risk listening to the point where we're unable to
make our mark. We risk listening to an extent where we are
unable to elevate beyond basic and toward brilliance. We risk
consuming the opinions others have about *us* twice as much as
we invest time in sharing our opinions with them. And *that* is a
big, fat, Greek-wedding-sized problem.

*If we follow the advice to listen twice as much
as we speak, we risk never getting a word in.
We risk not having the opportunity to be heard.*

#BIGDEALBOOK

Without going on a full-on fiery feminist rant, if you've ever
found yourself in a situation where you might have asked yourself, "Am I imagining this, or did he just cut me off for no reason?," or "Am I being nuts, or am I being interrupted every time
I talk?," or "Do I really have to speak more quickly to be able to
finish my full thought?," I'm here to tell you that (1) you are not
nuts and (2) "women being groomed to listen while men speak"
is Greek-tragically not new. In fact, sadly, it's even more ancient

than you might think. While researching the origins of this unfair airtime scenario in which we still find ourselves, I stumbled upon a pretty scary passage from, of all books, the *Bible*. While you may know that the Bible is typically a book many, myself included, rely on for a pretty solid life compass, what you might *not* know is what it says in the book of Timothy. Timothy 2:12 says: "I do not permit a woman to teach or to have authority over a man; she must be silent." I'm going to let that land here for a second. First of all, *seriously*? No way God believes that. There's just no way. Timothy probably didn't run that draft by the women in his life before publishing, either. Think of all the generations of robed-up dudes who thought God was giving them direct encouragement to be woman-shushing, shouty jerks? Sigh.

Fast-forward out of the Dark Ages when there were plagues and sexists, to modern day where thankfully both of those horrors have been wiped from the face of the earth . . . oh wait . . . and we find ourselves dealing with the modern-day machismo of what I call "down a peg" praise. An example of this you may have encountered lately? Receiving glowing adulation for your "soft skills." Like how we are better listeners than men. Or, that we are more empathetic, open to constructive criticism, genuinely interested in other perspectives, and thrive on collaboration. But the problem arises when you find that perhaps you've become *such* an adept listener, that you're actually *way* overdelivering on your Greek philosopher-recommended listening quota. And I'm not just talking about when you are fake-listening to people in your organization who love to hear the sound of their own voice. When we aren't intentional about whom we are listening to, we are left "all ears" but incredibly vulnerable to all sorts of major momentum-stopping pitfalls!

Listening too much to others' judgments and opinions over your inner GPS lady is the slowest route you can possibly select when you're traveling to your desired destination. And on a more extreme level, listening to haters and the venomous and malicious things they say, plot, or think about us is even more destructive to your momentum. Two ears to listen twice as much? Well, no offense, Epictetus, but if the ear-to-listening-time ratio were real—in a world where many women on the whole overlisten—some of us would have ears covering every inch of our bods!

Here's an audacious actuality: when it comes to others' unsolicited or excessively communicated negative opinions, listening can be lethal. Particularly if you are overlistening to why they don't agree, don't approve, don't understand, or just don't *like* your mission. Or your management style. Or your delivery style. Or your clothing style. Or whatever other area of your life they feel empowered and entitled to weigh in on, online or offline, because quite frankly, they hate it. Or you. Or both. Why? Well, in my home state of Maryland, when you put a bunch of crabs in a pot and one finds a way to start climbing out, the rest will immediately claw that enterprising crab right back down to face her impending doom with the rest of them. Nice try, hon.

Whether you're talking about actual or metaphorical crabs, haters are gonna hate. But the audacious woman has come to realize that it's high time those haters wait. It's time for them to wait until you've asked their opinion before they deliver it to you unsolicited. *Wait* until you've finished speaking. *Wait* until you've had a fighting chance to test this before they judge the results. When it comes to igniting or sustaining your momentum, the most mission-critical of tactics is a clear, audacious plan for dealing with your inevitable haters. And beware that that dislike of (*insert anything here*)—because there's always something—often disguises itself as "feedback," "constructive criticism," or "Can I give you a piece of advice?"

I have found there is one skill set we are not encouraged to cultivate, and yet it's one that has proved to be incredibly helpful to staying the course I have charted on major projects, big goals, and mental health in the toughest of times: becoming a worse listener. I know this sounds slightly insane in a "feed the flames of narcissism" way. And to be clear, I'm certainly not suggesting that the key to your success is to evolve into a shouty, interrupting foghorn that no one wants to be around. Or someone who isn't open to a trustworthy truth-teller setting you straight. I'm just saying that sometimes, when it comes to your haters, it's OK to hear with your ears, but you don't have to listen with your heart.

So how do you know if you're dealing with a well-meaning truth-teller or someone who's slugging pints of ice-cold lemon-lime Haterade? How can you tell who wants to elevate you and who wants to drag you back down into that Old Bay–scented, boiling pot? Let's reveal a few "innocent" questions and comments that are actually screaming identifiers that you are dealing with a potential (often well-intentioned) hater. The next time someone poses any of the following inquiries to you (of course, tone and context matter), raise a little red mental flag to be intentional about how much weight you decide to let the person's opinions hold with you. Because contrary to the classic business advice, for a female professional in any industry, sometimes the fastest way to crush it more is to listen less.

HATER HIT LIST

1. **The Nosey Hater**

   "Why aren't you married?"

   "Why are you getting married?"

   "Why are you single?"

   "Why don't you have children?"

   "Why don't you own a home?"

   "Why would you buy a house?"

   "You're going to work *and* raise your children?"

   "Why are you working instead of having children?"

   "You're only raising children and not working?"

   "You're outsourcing childcare?"

   "You're not going to college?"

   "Why would you go to college?"

   "You're starting your own venture?"

   "Why are you working for someone else?"

2. **The Condescending Hater**

   "Actually, that's a great idea/good point . . ."

   "Can you tone it down a little?"

"That's just not the way we do it."

"You wouldn't really understand what we're doing."

"You probably don't know this *but* . . ."

"That's *actually* not too bad because . . ."

"Sweetie, honey, sugar," or any other dessert-related name as an opener.

"Awwww. That's OK. You just need to . . ."

"You did great, considering (last time) (your tight timeline)."

3. The Small-Minded Haters

"You can't be serious."

"That can't happen in real life."

"Ha! That's cute."

"You're such a dreamer."

"That will never work."

"You can't just do that."

"Good luck with that one (sarcasm)."

"Zero chance of your plan working."

Beware that the most horrendous of haters are the ones who throw the sliest of the shade. Ignoring them is paramount if you want to push through the point where you keep getting stuck on a project, a goal, a life change, or chasing down your dream. And when it comes to winning the "make sure that everyone loves your life" game—spoiler alert—that ain't gonna happen, friend. It's the most unwinnable of games.

On the one hand, you have the more traditional expectations left over from our parents' (and older) generations including: get married when you're 25, give them grandchildren by 30, buy a house, know instinctively the certain way to do traditions, holidays, vacations, schools, and everything else. On the other hand, you have a more free-flowing, "just do you" forward-looking set of lifestyle expectations. And everything and everyone in between with individual expectations and perspectives—and the judgment that goes with them.

> *When it comes to winning the "make sure that everyone loves your life" game—spoiler alert—that ain't gonna happen, friend. It's the most unwinnable of games.*
>
> #BIGDEALBOOK

People always have an opinion, and most of them want everyone else to know (and react) to theirs. Just look at what happens when you post a decisive opinion on social media about *anything*. If you don't post, just imagine you updated your status to: "I voted for [*name*]." You can pretty much guess the range of raging responses that would come rolling on in. Is it any wonder that people post so much about their breakfasts when avocado toast is the only thing left we can all agree on? When it comes to you, your thing, or your dreams, they love you; they hate you; they don't understand you; they copy you; they don't get you; they want to copy you again.

For example, Lady Gaga was *so hated* for chasing her musical dreams in college that some of her peers started a Facebook group called "Stefani Germanotta You Will Never Be Famous." Imagine how you'd feel upon discovering that your classmates resented you that much. What did Gaga do when she saw that hate group? She ignored it. She audaciously didn't listen to what her peers had to say about her dreams. But what if she had believed them? What if she had altered her behavior to be a well-liked "popular girl"? What if she had let her unwillingness to shock or offend others muffle her talent? Well, she would never have become the first woman in history to win an Oscar, Grammy, BAFTA, and Golden Globe—all in *one year. That* is the power of audacity. (And pipes and guts and massive creativity, but still.)

But audacity comes in handy in our daily struggles, too—not just in the quest to the red carpet. When COVID-19 hit, lots of us lost gigs, jobs, trips, milestones, money, nest eggs, and dreams. A force we had nothing to do with robbed us of what we had been working *so hard* for. We were tripped by something that wasn't our fault—and that truly sucks. If Tracy Turnblad* can iron her hair, ignore the mean girls, and use her moxie to go from outsider to trendsetter, so. can. you. And if you can survive months in quarantine without actually going insane, you sure as heck can do *the thing*.

So what move in the game of life have you been hesitating to make because you're afraid *someone* will hate the player?

---

* From *Hairspray*—the movie, not the Aqua Net.

HURRY UP AND WAIT

If you had a dollar for every time you heard people say during the COVID-19 pandemic, "Well, as soon as things go back to normal . . . ," how wealthy would you be right now? Personally, I would be a multimillionaire typing this from my private island. Like hospitality and other industries disproportionately affected by the pandemic, the live events business came to an LA-traffic-jam-style, sudden, screeching halt. My fellow speaker friends who make a living preaching change found themselves in the uncomfortable position of having to take their own advice. Suddenly, instead of blasting out their strategies on adaptability, resilience, grit, strength, and other motivational topics, they had to walk their talk and apply their classic ideals to their new reality. But sometimes it really is easier to be a coach than a player. Especially when the game is about running as fast as you can with no end in sight.

Quickly, I saw some people wait, while others chose to create. The "Waiters" decided to wait for a vaccine, wait and see what everyone else decided to do, wait until the pandemic "ended," wait for a return to "normal." They took a decidedly negative tone on social media. They were despondent on Zoom. They lamented the past. The Waiters *hated* everything about this situation. When people would try to cheer them up, or make positive suggestions or uplifting insights, they would shoot them down. They didn't want to *hear* it. They had finally figured out their dream career, worked for decades to build it, and now were being forced to reinvent. A blow to be sure, and one that I certainly wasn't immune to.

On the other hand, given the exact same set of circumstances, some of my author/speaker/coaching friends revved right into Creator mode. The "Creators" rolled up their sleeves, put their chins up, and got to *work*. They cleaned out their garages and basements and built video-production studios. They learned how to light and shoot and edit. They created online courses. They reinvented their messages to be more relevant in the revamped landscape. They created new income trickles with coaching and consulting. The Creators executed new ways of connecting with their audiences virtually. They began intentionally removing negative players and voices from their lives and surrounding themselves (safely) with positivity and ingenuity and "yes and"-ers to reinvent their entire business. Some even did it from scratch because they had absolutely no other options.

Slowly, I watched as the Waiters admitted defeat and updated their LinkedIn profiles with their résumés. I watched as they ranted and raved online about whatever topic they could channel their frustrations into for that day. I watched as they pretty much self-imploded. Simultaneously, I watched as the Creators eked out maybe only a percentage of the revenue they were used to making, but, hey, it was better than zero! I watched as the Creators kept on keeping on. They audaciously blocked, unsubscribed, unfollowed, and *ignored* the Waiter-Haters.

Fast-forward a few months, and many Creators have said surprisingly they are really enjoying running their businesses from home instead of airports and hotels. One friend is really getting to know his children for the first time in years. Yet another is really enjoying updating his space. Another got some furry friends. Another said her marriage has never been better. Another said she is making more money for less work with a new product offering. Maybe you're a Creator with your own silver lining story. Maybe you're a Waiter turned Creator who is ready to write one. As a reformed Waiter myself, there's no shame in admitting that maybe you are long overdue to take a page out of the Creator book. Maybe you can experiment with a new routine, product line, or client target. What if you explored developing a new playbook or embracing a fresh mindset? What if you audaciously explored a completely new avenue of work, industry, or customer base?

So if you've been looking for a sign . . . maybe this is the one you've been waiting for.

"HOW DARE YOU" HATERS

Have you ever had a client, boss, or partner that continually doubted your abilities? Maybe they were constantly telling you what you "couldn't" or "shouldn't" do? Or for whatever reason, was this individual or team member just not a fan? I've been there, too.

I'll never forget when we landed one of our very first "big fish" social media clients for my marketing agency Socialite. My team and I flew up to San Francisco for the big kickoff meeting, and when we arrived, I felt like we were basically slow-motion strutting through the sparkling lobby. We had quite literally *arrived*.

As someone's assistant's assistant's assistant handed us our vegan cruelty-free organic Starbucks lattes, I gasped at the floor-to-ceiling views of the Golden Gate Bridge from every glass conference room. I remember shivering with excitement and anticipation because this was going to be the *best* client ever!

But as the dozen stone-faced executives rolled in, I could sense something was off. As we presented our carefully prepared creative ideas, instead of the usual client drooling with approval, each concept seemed to annoy them more. As we took the punches and pivoted our strategy on the fly, they rolled their eyes and stifled yawns. Everything about the way they treated my team and me telegraphed, *We are Goliath, and you are David minus the slingshot. And don't you dare spill that organic Starbucks.*

On the plane home, I brushed off my unease, telling myself first impressions are never the best. How many times have you had a rocky start and gotten projects back on track? It would be great! Looking back, I should have remembered the great Maya Angelou's advice that "when someone shows you who they are, believe them the first time."

As the contract wore on, I found myself getting the Sunday Scaries before our Monday meetings. (You know the Sunday Scaries, that paralyzing feeling of anxiety and dread over what Monday might bring?) With every "You're a replaceable vendor" brush-off comment and email, I grew more and more despondent. The harder my team worked and the more effort we put in, the more Goliath scorned us. We could have brought the client an extra $900 billion in revenue, and the people we were dealing with still wouldn't have even cracked a smile. They were truly a miserable bunch of grumps trying to find ways to drag others down to face their doom. Classic crabs in a pot scenario. To call this client unpleasant would be an understatement for the ages. And it was sucking all the joy out of my job and, even worse, making my poor team feel like total crap. Resonating for you, perhaps?

One day, a particularly salty San Franciscan shot off a rude email to my new marketing manager critiquing her work so harshly that she came to my office in tears. That was the last straw. Furious, I typed out one of those emails that you're supposed to save in your draft folders and sleep on it before you send it. You know the type? Yeah . . . except I accidentally sent it. Well, that poked the giant and ignited a chain of events that can only be described as a Fortune 100–branded dumpster fire.

In our final in-person meeting, as the fires raged and smoke billowed, one exec said for the umpteenth time that my team was no longer "allowed" to do something. And to make it worse, he started off the conversation with "How dare you. . . ." I accepted the unintended dare and fired him and his brand that *no one* fires. I slo-mo strode out of that Golden Gate war zone like Lara Croft. And as the smoke billowed behind me, I realized that sometimes the "You can't do that, how dare you" haters are the ones who actually make it the easiest for you to say, "Actually, yes we can." Dare accepted. You see, no matter how "big a deal" people or companies think they are, they're never so big that they deserve to be heard when what they're spewing is laced with toxic hostility.

Now I'd like to say that afterward, I felt dynamically recharged and never regretted my tomb-raiding bravado for a minute. But that's not what happened. After I calculated the hole in our revenue that dumpster fire had burned in my business, I curled up in a ball and cried and cursed my impetuosity to the highest heavens. I was regretful and pretty sure I had made a monster miscalculation. And I'll be honest; it was a pretty hairy couple of months recovering that revenue. But after enough time passed and the smoke cleared, we scored new clients that were a better fit. Clients that were respectful and weren't constantly projecting their unnecessary hostility and loathing.

So if you're in a situation where you are faced with the fanciest haters in the form of clients or bosses who are doubting your dynamic capabilities, depending on how hard you've worked to try and iron things out, there is a certain beauty in knowing when to stop listening and start walking. Because if those people are making everyone on your team miserable, they are not always right. And if you're in this situation right now, remember no amount of money is *ever worth* getting treated like crap. No amount of marquee-client panache is worth the dipping morale of you or your team. No amount of politics playing is ever worth feeling less than. Or unseen. Or unheard. Or disrespected. There are too many fantastic companies, teams, and people out there whose vibe better aligns with your authentic self and values.

Are there people you are working with, have hired, or teamed up with where it's really not working, but you feel like you "just can't" break up with them? Or walk away? Or cancel? But what if you did? What is the worst that could happen? More important, what is the best that could happen? Because no amount of money is ever worth hating what you do in a way that consumes your life. Sure, it might sting at first. You will likely second-guess yourself with fiery remorse, but ultimately, once all is said and done and you give the situation the time, space, and grace you need to see it clearly—you will feel so much more certain that where you are investing your precious time, energy, and brilliance is with individuals who appreciate and deserve to be in your outstanding orbit. Because after all, you're . . . *what*? Let me hear you! Yep, you're kind of a Big Deal. And BDE attracts other BDE. Life's too short. Pull the ripcord.

TRASH THE TROLLS

If you've ever announced anything in the online world—whether it was as big as sharing your new gig, promotion, award, or client, or something as vapid as showing off your new outfit or haircut—and been on the receiving end of negative digital feedback, you know those feels totally suck. Those feels of being shook up. Nervous. Disappointed. Embarrassed. Wanting to delete the post because of other people's response to it. Even though they have nothing better to do with their time than tear you down or try to entice you into engaging in a futile Facebook fight.

Or let's talk about offline, where you are rehearsing a presentation, practicing your art, or spearheading a function: no matter what it is, people who have no skin in the game, who haven't invested any effort in any of it, invariably have something to say. About what is missing, what they don't like, or what *they* would do. Sigh.

Spectators on the sidelines, critics, and commentators all have something in common: they weren't audacious enough to take the stage and do it themselves. So as we've talked about, their big reactions are oftentimes a reflection of how small your audacious actions made *them* feel. If you look stunning in a photo, maybe it was their jealousy that spawned that passive-aggressive comment. If you announce you launched your new venture, maybe it's an unwelcome reminder to them that the excuses they've been telling themselves about why they haven't done *their* thing are actually completely null and void.

The online disinhibition effect is a phenomenon observed by psychologists to explain why we behave in ways online that are ruder, more offensive, and more aggressive than how we behave in person. They attribute it to factors like physical distance, a delay in response times, and a lack of nonverbal feedback that lower inhibitions and empower people to say and do things they wouldn't have the guts to do in real life. It's a scientifically backed fact that most voyeurs are also haters. In other words, they aren't in the game. They are digital spectators, and they do *not* get a seat at the table of your life.

I'll never forget seeing John Krasinski, aka Jim from *The Office*, when he started his Some Good News network to offer moments of human hope, humor, and kindness when the pandemic first began. Millions and millions of people loved it. And then there were those other 4,000 people. They gave the thumbs down to good news. Heartwarming tales of snuggly puppies and helping the elderly, and *4,000* internet troll haters. My friends, if John Krasinski, aka Mary Poppins's husband, cannot avoid the haters, no one can. But he doesn't listen, and neither should you.

SOMEONE'S SHOT OF WHISKEY

There are haters who will judge how you get stuff done, because they wish they could get stuff done that way, or they're mad they didn't think of it first, or it just annoys them because they think their process, method, or approach is simply superior to all others. And when that ultimate knowledge is challenged? Well, they get a little . . . annoyed.

A few years ago, I sadly had to attend a family funeral, which meant taking off both Monday and Friday from my corporate job for travel days. As is Murphy's law of work, when you have all the time in the world, nothing is super-urgent. It's only when you have compressed bandwidth, that everything is suddenly due yesterday. So, I had three business days to complete five days of projects. I got to work with fairly low hopes for success but the craziest thing happened. With the urgency, no plan B, and forced focus—everything *somehow* got done! So not only was it possible to do a week's worth of projects in three days, but more important as a salaried mid-level employee, I had just reclaimed extra time that I didn't know I had previously been wasting!

After a week or two back on my old schedule, I decided to test the experiment again. I eased into Monday (no morning meetings) and eased out on Friday (no afternoon meetings), completing the bulk of what I needed to make happen in three action-packed hustle-mania mega-long days. It was a *game-changer*. I began sharing this new efficiency hack with my friends and a few trusted coworkers, dubbing it the "T2T" method, meaning you work in an überfocused, hyperefficient, change-the-world way Tuesday through Thursday, but you ease into and out of your weekend time for less harsh takeoff and landing. T2T is my own version of work-life balance in a way, because you are spending half your time focused on work and half on what you really want to be doing—with the same results as slogging through at a medium speed for five business days.

Think of it this way: You walk into the week Monday morning. Jog Monday afternoon. Sprint T2T. Jog Friday morning. And by Friday at noon? You are walking yourself into your family time, friend time, dog time, or *you* time. If you want to try it, you can start by calendar blocking so that you schedule all your toughest meetings, crush your most important discussions, tackle your biggest projects, and ignite your new initiatives T2T only. I try not to do any meetings on Monday or Friday unless absolutely necessary, and even then, only on Monday afternoon or Friday morning. The bonus? Your clients, coworkers, and even sometimes—secretly—your bosses are so much happier when they have their Monday mornings and Friday afternoons to transition between their own professional and personal lives. It's an audacious yet effective way to infuse more balance into how you invest your most important asset.

So I'd been living the T2T strategy for years now as a small business owner with serious success when I was asked to give a talk on social media at a conference. While talking about content planning and digital efficiencies, I casually mentioned my little T2T philosophy, and it was met with two very strong types of responses. Twenty percent of the feedback was seriously negative! (You yourself might be rolling your eyes or protesting such an absurd recommendation.) A few people got up and walked out of the room, rolling their eyes and muttering. Yet, the rest of the audience was totally loving it and gave me glowing reviews afterward. To this day I still get messages on LinkedIn about how much people love and still follow the T2T lifestyle.

The point is, anytime you're doing anything new, different, radical, or actually *interesting*—you're going to get people who *love* it and people who *hate* it. And one of the happiest moments in your life is when you unlock the audacity to let them love you or hate you without letting them get to you. Remember, it's not that you don't care what they think about your choices; it's just that you care *more* about what you think. If you have an operating strategy that works for you, yay if people get it! And if they don't, I guess they aren't your people. It's like my Irish nana always told me, "It's better to be someone's shot of whiskey, than everyone's cup of tea, love." Which are you?

WHEN THE HATER IS YOU

Sometimes, the hater you need to ignore the most isn't someone from your work life, your family, or your friend group. It's the hardest of the haters to ignore: the poisonous voice inside your own head. When you're your own internal Regina George, and your daily thoughts could make up a self-written mental *Burn Book*, it's fairly impossible to be your best self. Reprogram our inner Regina we must, for she is the most deceptive and deadly of all the haters.

Question: If the people who love you very much heard how you talk to yourself, what would they say? Would they be horrified? Defensive? Maybe a little concerned? How would you feel actually telling them what your inner self-talk sounds like? Did you just grimace a bit thinking about it? Hear me on this for a second: if you struggle with speaking to yourself in ways that you wouldn't speak to your worst enemy, you are not alone. Even the world's most confident women operating at the highest levels of success struggle with this. Even women whose job it is to literally study and specialize in coaching thousands of women around the world about their limitless possibilities.

One day, I was talking to my friend Laura Gassner-Otting, who wrote an incredible book called *Limitless* and cohosts a weekly room with me on Clubhouse. LGO, as she is called, is a former Clinton administration strategist and an incredible speaker, athlete, mom, wife—she's the real deal. She's from Boston by way of Miami, so from a double geography standpoint, let's just say she has no problem speaking her mind. So we were riffing one day about keynote optimization techniques when she confessed she really wanted to experiment more with "ranting." Meaning, instead of perfectly preparing her presentation from takeoff to landing, she would build in "rant time," which is essentially passionate spitballing on the fly. It might be incredible. It might be crap. It might shock. It might offend. And it's definitely audacious. She had mentioned that she had been dying to try it for months, but she just couldn't. I mentioned that hey, if Gary Vee (an entrepreneur whose personal brand consists of being brash, outspoken, and a tad controversial) can do it, "why can't you?" And without hesitating, she started laughing and said, "Well, Erin, c'mon. I'm no Gary Vee!"

I felt like the mind-blown emoji in real life. What the actual? This woman has a *way* more impressive résumé, and her platform and stage presence are captivating. Sure, I'm a Gary Vee fan, but this gal can *totally* match his star power onstage. I started sputtering to the point that she said, "OK, OK, I'll try it." And after her first "ranting" experiment, she called me, and guess what? Standing freaking ovation. You guys, if the author of a book about being limitless struggles with negative self-talk and impostor syndrome, is it any wonder that *of course* we mere mortals do as well?!

So the next time you're beating yourself up for stutter-stepping, remember that even the world's most confident, competent women—who teach confidence and competence *for a living*—question if they have what it takes to do what they dream! *raises hand* They wonder if they can deliver on what they really want to do. Let that sink in. If *they* question themselves, what does that mean for the rest of us? It means we have to *dig deep and believe* in our abilities. Believe that we are as qualified—*if not more so*—as others to do what we know we must. What we know we can. You are *not* an impostor; you are a talented individual that deserves to take up space. You deserve to be here. You deserve to be heard. You deserve to confidently operate like the Big Deal that you *know* you are. After all, feeling like an impostor is just an indicator of how much you *care* about overdelivering. And the reality is that those who never suffer from even the littlest bit of impostor syndrome? Well, it turns out they are typically the biggest impostors of all.

Even the world's most confident, competent women—who teach confidence and competence <u>for a living</u>—question if they have what it takes to do what they dream!

So when you walk into your next high-stakes scenario with your BDE on full display, remember: even if it (not you) bombs, even if it (not you) sucks, even if it's less than your most shining moment, you must audaciously get back up and *do it again anyway*. And again. And again. And delight in that again because every "again" is another rep you got in, a "repping stone" if you will, on your path to the greatness you were destined for. This is the defining factor between those who keep talking about it and those who are living it. Whenever that gremlin voice inside you is telling you that you're not ready to do, not qualified to do, not talented enough to do, you ignore that gremlin. You tell it to kiss your audacity. Because you *are* ready. You are qualified and talented enough right now. You have the BDE you need to surprise even yourself with what you are capable of. Because you can. (And if you can't, at least you'll know for sure because at least you had the grit to try.)

⇒ BIG DEAL DIARY ⇐

As we reach this point in the chapter, I want you to remind yourself to leave the hate and judgment and impostor syndrome untruths *out* of this diary sesh. Please be *kind* to yourself and don't fall into the self-hater trap as you complete this section. Please don't let the emotion of thinking about the haters in your life stop you from getting out onto paper everything you need to put their influence behind you so you can listen less and express more. As you read through the following questions, listen to yourself for the first answers that come to mind for you. Write your answers freely, without judging:

✳ Whom might you need to listen to less or ignore completely in your personal or professional life? Why?

✳ Which types of haters sounded familiar to you? What might you say to yourself to remind yourself to ignore them?

✳ If you have negative self-talk going on, what do you say to yourself most often? Can you commit to ignoring her and doing it anyway? When might be the next opportunity for you to do so?

#BIGDEALBOOK

CHAPTER 5

FEEL JEALOUS TO FIND GENIUS

She strutted out onto the stage wearing a skin-tight, black leather, long-sleeved jumpsuit with over-the-knee, sky-high, black boots. She rocked a swingy blond bob and spoke eloquently in a clipped British accent. If she had said her name was Lady Catwoman, I wouldn't have been surprised in the least. Less than a minute into her talk, Lady Catwoman had the hundreds of typically "tough crowd" marketers attending this serious business conference laughing, clapping, and sitting on the edge of their seats, hanging onto her every word. Her real name? Cindy Gallop. Her superpower? In her exact words: "Blowing shit up."

The conference was taking place at a Walt Disney World resort, but in that moment, Cindy was taking us on a more exciting ride than anything Walt could have ever dreamed up. Amid presentations on digital trends and web analytics, she was talking about how the ubiquity of hard-core pornography had distorted young men's sexual education. In front of this majority male audience, she detailed her mission to improve healthy conversations around sexual behavior. She was the consummate definition of an awesomely audacious woman.

I was inspired; I was shocked; I was enthralled; I was . . . jealous. *Jealous?* What? I'm all for girl power! I'm all for sisters supporting sisters! How dare I feel jealous of Lady Catwoman doing what she was clearly born to do? Guilt and shame immediately replaced my envy as I joined the rest of the crowd in a thundering standing ovation for her brilliance and, quite frankly, balls.

Jealousy. The green-eyed monster. Most of us are taught from childhood that this terrible creature is to be slayed at all costs. And, yes, of course, jealousy that incites malice or spite or robs us of our contentment or gratitude for our blessings is the most poisonous of all emotions. "Thou shalt not covet" and those other nine rules from Above offer a rather solid road map for a life well lived.

And in certain moments, like Cindy's Wild Disney Ride, my jealousy was also my "genius." Genius in reference not to book smarts or intelligence but to intuition. That unconscious, unexplainable side we all have in us that just *knows better*. And in that moment, my genius was telegraphing a momentous message. Like it had just ripped a quick shot of jealousy juice, my conscious brain lowered its inhibitions and started shouting, *Hey! Quit trying to not feel what you feel! What Cindy just did up there on that stage? Yeah! You're meant to do that!* Have you ever felt like that? And I don't mean like a liquid courage–

induced competition with your coworker who just slayed "Lose Yourself" Eminem style at the team karaoke night.

Fast-forward five years, and my Lady Cindy Catwoman jealousy came in handy—*big time*. I was at a conference in Vegas that my agency was managing. Everything was going smoothly, until suddenly the client ran up to me fighting back tears because her social media speaker didn't show up for a breakout session. She was panicking because the session started in 30 minutes and the room was packed, and she asked would I please just get up there and talk to them?

Instead of melting down (OK, well, I fully melted down in the bathroom right after), I remembered Cindy Goshdarn Gallop. I remembered my jealousy. I remembered that genius feeling of just *knowing*. And I said yes. (Side note: Cindy Gallop would never, *ever* be uncool enough to use the word *goshdarn* in a sentence. Ever.) And while my J. Crew blazer and boring trade-show flats weren't *exactly* her Catwoman ensemble, I strutted to the front of that room, and I channeled my inner Cindy. I borrowed her attitude as I preached passionately about the esoteric, transformational topic of . . . Instagram profile design. And when I finished, the people in the audience rose to their feet—and left.

While I did not receive anything even remotely resembling a standing ovation, I received something even better: a handful of invites to speak at a few other events. One thing led to another, and before long, my full-time job somehow evolved into speaking on stages around the world—just like Lady Cindy Catwoman herself.

Can you imagine what could be possible if you allowed yourself to acknowledge the scandalous reality that maybe, *maybe*, your jealousy is actually not completely reprehensible? That maybe it's actually *your* genius speaking to you loud and clear on what you want? On who you were really meant to be?

If you've been saying to yourself, *I don't know how to do that!* or *I don't even know what I want!* or *I could never do that*, then as Lady Cindy Catwoman would say, *Bullshit.* Yes, you do. You do know how. You do know who. You do know where. In fact, as intuition is individual, you're actually the *only* one who knows how and who and where. The real question is, will you audaciously authorize yourself to receive what your jealously genius is air-dropping you? What are you "healthily jealous" of? A place? A job? A person? A mission? A mindset? A skill set? A lifestyle? What if you allowed yourself to scandalously recategorize a flash of envy as something to be honored, instead of a shameful emotion that "should" only be ignored?

As strange as it sounds, oftentimes that disgraceful, desirous feeling is actually a perfectly precise path to uncovering what it is your soul truly seeks. Allowing yourself to feel and dissect your *jealousy*? I know; it's almost as scandalous as talking porn at a professional convention. And just as worthy of a standing ovation when you do.

Now obviously there are *plenty* of times jealousy does not lead to discovering your true calling, and that's when you know you're dealing an emerald emotion of the poisonous variety.

UNHEALTHY JEALOUSY VERSUS HEALTHY JEALOUSY

So how do you know whether you should categorize your covetousness as super-Shero inspiring or just plain catty? Simple:

whether it's a one-off or a recurring visitor, are you *competing* or are you *comparing*? Maybe you've never really given the question much thought, but it's a distinction that makes all the difference.

Healthy competition can be an incredibly powerful motivator for getting you up off your butt or back in the saddle. Healthy competition is the fire you need to push yourself that last mile to transform your most audacious dreams into your new reality. On the other hand, unhealthy comparison is straight-up lethal poison to your mind, body, and soul. Unhealthy comparison will swallow you whole and completely rob you of every opportunity to relish in deep, true, lasting joy. You might think that sounds a tad dramatic, but I assure you it is without a shadow of doubt 10,000 percent accurate. And this dream destroyer, this joy stealer, this best-life blocker is precariously prevalent thanks to the normal pressures of not just your work life and home life but your digital life as well.

Let me ask you this: Do you really, truly, *genuinely* want to start inviting more joy, passion, and contentment into your everyday existence? If you said yes, I'd like to invite you to really rethink how you're (consciously or unconsciously) playing the world's most unwinnable games of keeping up with the Joneses. Or the Kardashians. Or the entire TikTok community, LinkedIn universe, or whatever corner of the internet you stack up your dance routines, family photos, or professional accolades against. You and I (and the rest of humanity) find ourselves involuntarily(ish) ensnared within the confines of an extremely risky social experiment at a global scale. If you haven't established a way to *actually* stop measuring your real life against everyone else's highlight reel, versus just *saying* "You know their posts aren't the whole story"—you will continue to feel less than, empty, and not enough, no matter how much other work you put in. Full stop.

Now, I'm not going to sit here and tell you exactly *how* to stop comparing against another person's promotion, salary, tenure, golden parachute, or Pinterest-perfection home—that's something only you can decide to do. Only you can resolve to once and for all stop measuring yourself by the *world's* yardstick and start to measure yourself by *your own*. Competition can be a terrific power source, but comparison will almost always drain your battery.

Competition can be a terrific power source, but comparison will almost always drain your battery.

#BIGDEALBOOK

So how do you know whether or not your jealousy is actually a genius way to prompt yourself into a little healthy competition?

HEALTHY COMPETITION IN ACTION

You'll know healthy competition is in action when you find yourself quite literally mouth-open exhilarated by someone else's success—filtered or unfiltered. You see the person's wins, and you're fired up to go chase down some points for your own board.

When you see that person crushing the project, the workout, the fund-raiser, or the quota, your organic reaction is some version of "Go, you!" immediately followed by a hearty, energized "Now, let's go, me!" If you had to explain healthy competition in a text to yourself, it would be the emoji love child of "hands clapping" and "cool sunglass face."

You know it's healthy competition when someone positively provokes you to work harder, dig deeper, and go beyond your current stretch point. When the person has affected you to level up your everyday efforts in ways you just weren't doing solo. When you find yourself undoubtedly galvanized to pick up your pace a tad from where you were yesterday.

A little competition can help raise more money for cancer research. A little competition could mean seeing that super-fit 65-year-old with the rock-hard triceps in Orangetheory Fitness who inspires you to press that + button on your speed or incline. A little competition can propel you forward for that one last sales call or help you show up with extra BDE for that one last meeting to finish the quarter stronger than you thought possible.

When it comes to unhealthy competition, you'll know you're veering off in the wrong direction when you find that you're comparing yourself to others in a way that amplifies your deepest, darkest, "not-enoughness." You may not even realize that you're inviting in such a toxic, self-worth-decimating behavior. It's sneaky like that. What might happen if you paid closer attention to those occasions when you're feeling insecure, when you find your self-talk crossing over from positive reinforcement

(*OK! Let's see if I can improve a bit here!*) to negative reinforcement (*Ugh! I look/feel/sound vile today.*)?

One evening my neighbor Margot and I were walking together after work and she confided that she was in total awe of two of our other friends. Was it because of their new subway tile backsplashes? Their shiny new Beamers? Nope. She was in awe of something much more valuable, much more luxurious, much more precious: a standing one-hour coffee-talk date that transpired every weekday morning at 10:30 a.m. Why was something as basic as a coffee date so jaw-droppingly, awe-inspiringly fabulous? Well, Margot worked a nine-to-five corporate HR job that required her to be in the office, in a cube, working on a dusty old PC, every weekday, no matter what. From where she sat, chained to the comfort of her paycheck and 401(k), a midmorning coffee-talk break seemed like a luxurious privilege reserved for the überwealthy stay-at-home moms with nannies, personal trainers, and fur-and-diamond-encrusted toilet paper.* When the two friends would burst out laughing later recalling one of their coffee talks, Margot always found herself biting her lip in an attempt to curb the flow of FOMO. She was curious. She was wistful. She was *way jealous*. She found that she couldn't help but wonder what that kind of flexible work schedule would be like, what that type of professional freedom would *feel* like, what that kind of coffee would even *taste* like!

Her two gal pals were both small business owners. Maybe you know one; maybe you are one. Either way, picture two typical, classic, mad-respect, rise-and-grind entrepreneurs. One

---

* Never out of stock, even during a pandemic.

owned a small digital marketing shop, and the other ran a mobile hair-removal/spray-tan business. They both worked their butts off to get their companies off the ground, and they both worked like maniacs in the mornings and afternoons—and most evenings. But like smart entrepreneurs who know it's a marathon and not a sprint, 10:30 to 11:30 in the morning was blocked off for their sacred recharge sanity time.

Now, Margot could have caved into her caveman comparison impulse to determine her hierarchy within the tribe. She could have stayed wallowing in the safe yet sucky pond of "poor me—why not me" jealousy. She could have sloshed around feeling sorry for herself being stuck in the tedious, buzzword-laced meetings she abhorred at that exact time every single day. She could have easily snuggled into that same-old, cozy-old, familiar, negative "wahhh" narrative.

Instead, she chose to look at her two friends as her own personal supply chain of healthily competitive energy. She noted how they were operating, Blue Steel–stared at herself in the mirror, and said *Let's go, me!* Instead of making excuses for why they could do it and she couldn't, she got radically real and leveled with herself. Her mantra became "Well, if they somehow figured it out, why can't I?" She started researching what might be possible for her and how she might start her own venture in the future. Did she have a burning desire to solve a specific problem? Not really. Did she have a *Shark Tank* idea she was totally obsessed with? Nope. All she knew was that her definition of success was not the money, the fame, or the challenge—it was the freedom. Success to her was attaining the simple goal of having the freedom for a 10:30 morning coffee talk with her friends. She didn't want to choke down one more cup of corporate drip sludge. Her dream was to level up to a vanilla latte with almond milk and a sprinkle of cinnamon on top, thank you very much.

Fast-forward two years, and there was Margot, sprinkling that cinnamon on top with a huge BDE smile on her face. She was now the one saving the best table at the coffee shop for the three of them. Of course, before and after coffee talk, she is working her tailfeather off with her new HR/payroll consulting firm she launched. She doesn't have dreams of blowing it up to make billions and be acquired. She doesn't want the headache of payroll and staff. She's not trying to disrupt the hiring process for the next generation. She's just building a small, manageable, enjoyable lifestyle business that supports her dream of Starbucks ladies gab time on her own terms. But the beauty of Margot's approach is how she chose to process, observe, and *leverage* her friends' success. She transformed what could have been an audacity blocker into an audacity activator. She took her jealousy juice, ran it through the purifier, and chugged it. Was she scared? Overwhelmed? Worried? Lost? Did she second-guess herself? Yes! Of course! Duh! But for her, all of that faded away when she woke up in the morning without the feeling of prisoner reporting for trash pickup.

So . . . what about you? When you look at the Starbucks sisters in your life who are crushing it—at work, love, health, mindfulness, stress management, sales goals, or whatever haunts you—do you feel more *Why not me?* or *Let's go, me?*

Now, of course, your answer is likely a blend of both, depending on the person, the situation, and whether or not

Mercury is in retrograde. (Why is it *always* in retrograde?) Your answer might depend on how full your emotional bank account is at that particular moment. If the truth is that you find yourself feeling like "you're behind" or "you're not as successful/skinny/wealthy/[*insert whatever adjective comes to mind here*]"—first of all, don't judge yourself on top of feeling your feelings. Nothing is wrong with you. You are not crazy. You are not insecure. You are just a typical, regular, "look around to see what's up" human like the rest of us.

Nothing is wrong with you; you're just succumbing to the classic complication of living in this new, hyperconnected world like pretty much everyone else. Without an intentional digital health strategy, it's almost impossible *not* to fall into a caveman comparison conundrum as our default. If my cave neighbor has Fire 2.0, I *must* have Fire 3.0! But just because that's how most of today's carefully curated newsfeed cave people are scrolling through life, that doesn't mean you have to get sucked in too.

Look, I'm not asking you never to compare yourself to anyone again for the rest of your life. Let's be honest; that's just not realistic or feasible. What I am asking you to do when you feel this comparison crap start to cramp your style is to remind yourself of your BDE. Remind yourself that you rock. Remind yourself that your life rocks right now and that it will rock even more in the future. Remind yourself that you rocked your day with all the fierceness, fire, and fab you could muster and you totes crushed it. And when you're swimming with that spirit of "yay, you!," you'll find it much easier to drastically *reduce* the time you spend playing the world's most unwinnable of games and dramatically increase the time you spend keeping your eyes on your own paper and being *stoked* by what you see there. Basically, be a little bolder when it comes to telling yourself that you really are a gem. That you already have exactly what it takes to pull the trigger on at least the first step toward chasing down what it is you long for.

Be a little bolder when it comes to telling yourself that you really are a gem.

EVOLVE FROM COMPARING TO COMPETING

Now, I know what you're thinking: *Erin, I've seen the Pinterest "Comparison is the thief of joy" posts. I've liked "The only person you should compare yourself to is you" stories. I've sipped from that glittery coffee cup reminding me "Don't compare your beginning to someone else's middle."* I have, too. So I'm not going to sit here and retweet these same tired adages at you, for three very specific reasons. (And *no*, one of the reasons is *not* that you can just go buy the preceding platitudes artfully burned into old barnwood in my Etsy shop. Although if that is one of the businesses you've been jealous of, this is your "sign" to start your shop.)

First, when you hear someone say "Stop comparing yourself to others," it's like when someone says, "Stop thinking about Liam Hemsworth shirtless." What do you think of? Exactly. (And you're welcome.)

A few years ago, I was backstage watching a super-fit key-note presenter before me give a fantastic talk encouraging us to stop comparing ourselves so much to our peers. Guess what happened next? Yep, in that less-than-ideal moment, I started comparing myself to her. And my speech to her speech. And my "taco lover" triceps to her "these guns haven't seen a carb since 01" ones. Cue the comparison spiral. You've been there, right? Like Alice in GunShowLand I went down the "hate myself" hole. And the more I told myself to stop, it was like it was having the opposite of the Liam Hemsworth effect. Instead of preparing my best "place of service" headspace with prayer, music, and more prayer—I went to the ladies' room and started doing that thing where you pinch your arms back to imagine what they would look like without those little lunch-lady wing things. Not exactly the smartest way to get pumped up. (Pun intended.)

So as you might imagine, when I took the stage, my takeoff was bumpier than a flight leaving the Windy City. Long silences where I usually got laughs, stuttering where I usually articulated clearly. My triceps and I were *tanking*. It took me almost half of my talk to shake off that insecure turbulence, get back in my zone, and focus on fulfilling the mission at hand. Thanks to one hype girl in the front row who was nodding her head enthusiastically (always find your hype girl!), I ended up working it out in the end, but let's just say my upper lip sweat sheen was definitely visible from the back row of the conference center.

Have you ever had that happen? When you told yourself to "stop" something, and it manifested and magnetized that exact behavior? Stop saying *like*! Stop buying crap you don't need from Amazon! *Like all I want now is like all of Amazon.*

Second, just telling yourself to "stop comparing" isn't the end-all, be-all vaccine to combat comparison because of how the world of social media is scientifically engineered. Social media is literally architected for voyeuristic comparison. It's strategically designed and continually optimized to be irresistible when it comes to seeing how we stack up with the rest of the world. It's "innocent limited human powers you" taking on the "not-so-innocent robot powers algorithm." If you've ever gotten that itch to check your phone when you know you shouldn't, you know the addiction is real. (Did you just think about it?) Who has more likes? Looks the best? Has the most followers? Endorphin hit! Pleasure ding! Serotonin shot! Don't think you have a problem? What's the first thing you do when you open your eyes in the morning? Hmmm . . .

Sure, social media can be a digital lifeline to combat loneliness when used appropriately to open new offline relationships and nurture long-distance ones. But even when you're using social platforms with the healthiest of intentions to simply stay connected, it still takes a mammoth effort to protect your headspace and heart space from the endless black hole scroll of curated perfection. One way to increase your chances of reprogramming your relationship with technology is to replace a stop with a specific start. When it comes to habit swapping, the magic really does lie in mapping out the details. For example, if you've ever tried to quit your nighttime snack, dessert, or glass of wine, you know it's much easier to stay the course if you have a healthier alternative on deck like that herbal tea or sparkling water mocktail. Rising above the power of the smartest minds in Silicon

Valley calls for a much more specific course of action than just a sparkly coffee cup quote.

Finally, when you say "Stop comparing and just be grateful for who you are and what you have," how does that impact the line between comparison-fighting gratitude and lame old complacency? If you are just "doing you"—aka being so grateful and content with where you are now; no matter what everyone else is up to, you're good, thank you very much—do you just drift into the waters of complacency? Do you just suddenly wake up one day and find that you are the captain of the USS *Mediocrity*? We're advised not to compare ourselves, but at the exact same time never to be complacent. Well, how do we maintain our edge professionally if we don't keep an eye on what's new and what everyone else is doing out there?

So, if both are unhealthy extremes, how the heck can we optimize toward living our best lives, especially in these complex times? Being candid, it is challenging, but it is *not* impossible. You *can* eradicate the negative and bear-hug the positive. Here are *four* specific techniques that pretty much always work for me and for my clients. It's my hope one of them might work for you too, or at least trigger your own version of comparison closure.

MIX YOURSELF A "GRATITINI"

This is one of my *go-to strategies* to halt comparison in its totally life-limiting tracks. When you scroll across something that ignites that feeling of "I'm not as [*whatever*] as she is," or you hear that inner gremlin start talking down to you—you turn your phone over, or throw it in a drawer, or put it under a pillow, and you physically walk away from your phone. You socially distance yourself from your device. You then close your eyes, and mix yourself a mental gratitude martini—a *gratitini*. Here's the recipe: it's three parts *radical* gratitude and one part eye-roll "Yeah, right. Insta is so fake" reality check.

While I'm optimistic that if you're reading this book, you already possess some type of gratitude practice in your daily routine, I'd like to invite you to level up from your typical thank yous to an intentional appreciation of the radical variety. What does this mean? Well, it means going galaxies beyond just writing or saying one of the go-to gratitude classics: *I'm so grateful for my partner, parents, children, health, job, house, shoes, coffee, breakfast, sunny day,* and so on. Where things get radical is when you don't move on until you *feel* the gratitude. The *feels* are *essential* to activate the awesome here.

I don't know about you, but for me, I had gotten to a point where my gratitude practice was like a to-do checklist where I brushed my teeth, threw in some laundry, or remembered to pluck that rogue black chin hair I saw in the rearview at that red light yesterday. (Pro tip: *always* keep tweezers in your glovebox. Stoplight natural lighting reveals all.) Where things got *radical* was when I started sitting with the word that I'd written or spoken until I *felt* the grateful feels. For me, either it's a shiver, or I start to feel a little choked up, like I could fully turn on the waterworks. For you, maybe it triggers a smile, a sense of calm, or a little flutter of excitement in your heart.

And the difference in this gratitude practice is remarkable. We're talking more patience with my husband, more creativity with my clients, and more thoughtfulness with my friendships. We're even talking better sales numbers because prospects can *feel* your radical gratitude good vibes. (You know when you like certain people, want to hire them, work with them, or just be their friend, but you can't put your finger on exactly *why*? Yep. Radical gratitude gal right there.) The secret here is you *have* to wait until something physical transpires. Sit with your thankful emotions until your body literally shows you that radical gratitude has transpired.

So you repeat this for *three things*. Why three? It just seems to be a manageable yet magic number for me, but if you're pressed for time, you can do one; or if you're feeling Tibetan monk–like, you can do it for ten or more. For me, it's three smiles, three shivers, or three fluttery heart moments. Your response is yours, but you will recognize when your personal "gratitude completed" notification comes through. You then flip your newly Zen mind back to the original perpetrator that made you feel less than and finish off the gratitini with a splash of eye-roll reality check. As in, "OK, you and I both know that pic was filtered and FaceTuned to the high heavens." Or "OK, *yes*, she got that job, but let's be real; she's going to have zero social life for the next three years." Or "OK, they look really happy, but you know for a fact that there's always more to the story of that 'perfect relationship' that's being projected."

Maybe you can't see behind the scenes of what is really happening, but you are getting only one small glimpse into what that person's reality is really like. So you bake this reality check reminder in with a super-immature and not so Zen (but highly effective) eye-roll. Or however you brush things off in a good-natured way. Sometimes, I'll sip a few gratitinis a day. Even before noon. It's a silly little mind trick that I use to release the very human and very natural yet simultaneously treacherous negativity. You mentally swirl, sip, and savor your gratitini until you feel yourself start to fill your energy back up with enough good vibes to go back to living positively with a stronger focus on your *own* mission. When you feel the audacious buzz of a gal back on track, then you can go retrieve your phone. And remember to smile at it in a "Nice try, but a Big Deal babe like myself knows better than that" kinda way.

YOU DO YOU

Have you ever had a moment where you were so embarrassed at how you behaved that it kept haunting you? Where every time you think about it, you just want to bury your face in a pillow and bargain with the universe for a do-over? And I'm not talking about that time in middle school when you laughed so hard you accidentally tooted in front of your crush. I'm talking a grown-up life "never live it down"–er.

I have.

Last year, I was at a dinner party at my friend Andrew's family home where he grew up in Laguna Beach. It was one of these super-unique, artsy, "if these walls could talk" abodes. I remember right before we scooted over there being *so* excited because my Instagram followers had finally hit 10,000, aka I had access to the "swipe up" feature! Now before you roll your eyes at this vapid achievement, if you are someone like me who relies almost 100 percent on social media to engage with your customers and clients, that is, to pay your bills, then you know the game-changing impact of being able to directly link to your products and services so you can monetize all your hard contenting work online. And you can only do this when you have reached the coveted 10,000-follower mark. So when I *finally* hit that delicious digital milestone, I was on Insta cloud nine!

After a few glasses of wine, I found myself humblebragging (just kidding, I was straight-up bragging) to one of Andrew's friends whom I had just met. His name was Dan, and he was soft spoken and very humble, and politely congratulated me on my newfound "mini-influencer" status. (Not that I needed any more congratulations, as I was doing a fairly good job of patting myself on the back.) Later, Dan and his equally humble and ridiculously cool wife, Sonny, had to leave early to relieve their babysitter. After they left, another one of Andrew's friends came up to me, not knowing what we had been talking about, and said, "You should really follow him on Instagram." Looking him up, I saw that humble, kind, under-the-radar Dinner Party Dan had almost a *million followers*. One. Million. I spit out my Malbec and had a "Cameron from *Ferris Bueller* after he wrecks his dad's fancy car" moment and just stared unblinkingly. I could not even speak.

It turns out when Dan told me he was a creative director for a "cool company in LA," that company was Marvel Comics. Dan was an incredibly talented artist who had amassed a huge die-hard fan base of his work, with each post having hundreds of thousands of likes and comments! I felt like such a self-obsessed, absurd, pompous *eejit*; I wished one of Dan's superheroes would swoop down and just carry me away. Not in a romantic "Save me" way but in a "Please remove me from here and drop me into the nearest out-of-the-way dumpster" one.

Upon this ego-murdering discovery, the wind left my sails. My shoulders slumped and I began to annihilate the charcuterie board. All of my joy completely vanished. (Well, not completely; the baked brie was pretty all-time.)

Seeing my nonverbal defeat and sadness, the guy who had unmasked Dan's literal superhero identity said, "Hey, cheer up! If you want to know the truth, I'm jealous of *you*. I have only 500 followers! I would *kill* to have 10,000. You're so lucky!" And in that moment, I was struck with really understanding a truth that most of us know in our heads, but few of us really know in our hearts. The 500-follower guy would love to be the 10,000-follower gal, who would love to be the 1 million-follower dude. And Dinner Party Dan is probably chasing down someone else online who has 5 million followers!

What I realized and have never forgotten since that moment is whether we are talking about followers or anything else we value, we are all only human and *there is and will always be* someone who is [insert adjective: *better, richer, prettier, skinnier, smarter, more talented, better traveled, more successful,* whatever] than you. The world is a *really* big place. You know that, but do you really, really *know that*? And more important, do you know with even more conviction that there will also always be someone who is not as gifted as you? There will always be someone who doesn't have your gift of gab, your ability to think strategically, navigate conflict, crush the race, show tough love, radiate empathy, simplify the complex subject, or make even the Grinchiest of grumps burst out laughing. There are millions of people in this massive world who will never come *close* to possessing your special and unique and mind-blowing Big Deal talents.

The older you get and the more you travel and, yes, even scroll, the more you realize there are a dizzying number of successful humans doing grand, mind-blowing things, and *yay* for them! They are doing them, and you are doing you, and there is one thing that we all have in common: on our deathbeds, whether we changed the whole actual world or just the ones we created for ourselves, *none of us* will give two Marvel superhero *bam-pows!* about Instagram. (I invite you to pause and reread that sentence. And like radical gratitude, I encourage you to keep reading it until you physically *feel* it and *know* it in a way you can take this truth off these pages and into your life starting *right now*.)

The second thing I (days later) realized from my dinner party bragfest is that when we mere humans compare ourselves or allow ourselves to feel unhealthy jealousy, we are fighting thousands of years of programmed evolutionary behavior from all the way back to Fire 1.0 trying to figure out if our chances of survival were higher if we fought or backed down. So when you do it, give yourself a break. Know that we all slip up. And commit to sipping a gratitini to do better the next time.

When you choose to replace comparison with healthy competition, you unlock your chained-up inner audacity like Aladdin and his magic lamp. Your superpower is Robin Williams saying to you:

"Oh to be free, such a thing would be greater than all the magic in the world!" When you dare to free your audacity, it roars into your life ready to turn your words and wishes into a new reality that's fit for a Disney movie. It is actual, real-world magic. And it's at your disposal. It's on demand. It's lying there dormant just crossing its fingers waiting for the day you'll discover it and put it to work.

Of course, it's one thing to *know* this and another to *feel* it. Luckily for you there is one other way to trick your heart into feeling what your head already knows. You simply don a pair of bestie blinders.

DON YOUR BESTIE BLINDERS

I learned about bestie blinders from my friend Kim (we'll learn more from Kim in Chapter 7) back when I was living in Baltimore in my early twenties. Facebook had been out for only a few years, and I remember being over at her apartment and making a catty comment about a guy I had dated on and off who had posted a photo with his new babe of a girlfriend. (Who also happened to be a doctor. Seriously?)

This was back when *The Secret* by Rhonda Byrne was hugely popular, and Kim sagely advised me, "E! You need to be super-careful about the energy you put out in the world—even online. Vibes are like boomerangs. Whatever you put out there is exactly what you will attract back to yourself—times 10!"

Kim continued: "Just pretend that girl in the photo is me, and that I had found happiness with a new guy. Wouldn't you look at that photo and say, 'Good for her!' and mean it?"

"Yeah, of course," I grudgingly responded.

Kim, my annoyingly sage Yoda friend closed with, "Remember, happy people are happy for people."

At that moment her refusal to let me be a straight-up brat was extremely irritating, but looking back now, I'm beyond grateful for her advice. I never forgot that little mental switch to reroute my vibes from awful to abundant. That little flip of the script has saved me more times than I can count, and it will do the same for you.

The next time you come across someone, online or offline, who makes you feel those "I'm not good enough compared to her/him/them" feelings, *Why not me?*, you immediately—I mean *right away*—call to mind your absolute favorite person. If you find yourself having these feelings often, decide on who that person is right now, so the next time you start to feel the ugly feelings, you literally snap your fingers and call to mind that person you love. Who is it for you? Put that person on deck right now, so the negative comparison crap doesn't stand a chance of getting a solid foothold inside your audaciously prepared self. Maybe it's your best girlfriend, your sister, your mom, your cousin, your child, your partner. Whoever it is, visualize that one person you would literally die for. Then whatever is happening, being posted, or said, dare yourself to pretend that it's happening to your favorite person.

You pretend that the promotion, the new house, the vacation, the award is being experienced by your favorite person on earth. And you begin to trick your feelings into evolving from a negative *Why not me?* to a positive *good for her*. Because whatever wonderful thing, person, place is happening to your bestie, her joy is your joy. Her success is your success. And you'll be shocked as you watch how fast those negative comparison feelings will dissipate. You will find that, instead of biting your lip, picking your nails, or sighing with sadness, you've tricked your mind into smiling. You've tricked your mood into lightening. You've tricked your emotions into laughing.

And after you feel your emotional tide start to crash toward that healthier direction, you *move on*. You *don't* look back over your shoulder to dig anything back up—whether old pain or posts. Remember, like Kim said, vibes are like boomerangs. What you send out is what you attract back times 10. If you really want to reprogram these types of *Ugh! Why do I do this?* thoughts and feelings, bestie blinders will get you there every time.

DECIDE: TEAM ABUNDANCE OR TEAM SCARCITY?

Making sure your squad is packed with members of Team Abundance is yet another way to reroute your vibes from awful to abundant.

Prior to COVID, my everyday was hotel and airport hopping, going from keynote to keynote. Many of my dear girlfriends also live this unique, not-for-everyone "digital nomad" lifestyle. We spend hours on FaceTime, brainstorming everything from new speech material we're thinking about adding to our next talk to how to optimize status and points programs. When we're pumped post-keynote, we cheer, laugh, and support. When we're lonely on the road, we confess and cry. One crew in particular is a squad we call the SheNoters (a foursome composed of myself, Neen James, Tami Evans, and Tamsen Webster).

As you can imagine, a big part of how we grow our online tribes so we can increase our ability to influence change in the world is to introduce each other to our audiences (case in point with the previous SheNoters intro—notice how I plugged each of them?). We share each other's content, interviews, shout-outs, recommendations, and so on. This retweeting, reposting, and resharing comes from a steadfast belief in the "rising tide lifts all boats" mindset. Maybe your crew came to mind when I mentioned my SheNoters. If so, it's likely that your invisible girl power jersey would indicate that *you* are a member of Team Abundance. Sounds fab, right? It is. And most women on the planet, whether they realize it or not, are on one of these two teams: Team Abundance or Team Scarcity.

Team Abundance is stacked with audacious gals who hang with other audacious gals who are obsessed with helping each other live bigger, bolder lives in a way that we probably couldn't (or at least wouldn't want to) do alone. We are playing the game of life in a healthily competitive way. We're cheering each other on from the sidelines and then tagging each other back and forth into working our butts off out on the field. Yes, when you're on this team, you want to contribute your goals and assists just like the other team members did—if not more!—but all the efforts, energy, and enthusiasm count toward the same collaborative winning result. Your stats and their stats are all in the name of the collective win. There's an abundance of victory and glory to go around for everyone. Go team!

The other team is *Team Scarcity*. What's this team's deal? Well, this is a team that plays dangerous and dirty. Team Scarcity players talk trash. Every goal you score is one that should have been theirs. They aren't competing to see who is the better player; they're comparing to see who is the better person. Their style is ruthless, demoralizing, and divisive. After the game is over, let's just say they don't exactly shake hands with one another and say "Good game." Boo.

If you're dealing with some of these Team Scarcity players, I have an idea for you: take a look at those you surround yourself with or those you follow on social media and remove them now. Block and bless. Delete their number. Get rid of those bad vibes. And what do you do next? Replace them with new people to join your very own Team Abundance.

Making space to consume content from Team Abundance players who would elevate our "everyday," is *anything* but minuscule, absurd, and insipid. It is audacious. Is it "Bethany Hamilton going back out surfing after a shark ate her arm" audacious? Not even close. But removing those BDE suckers will make you feel so much lighter and happier and more grateful to be on your own path without them. Stop wasting energy comparing someone else's path so you can protect and project your BDE.

So as you mentally shuffle through the women in your life, sometimes it will be obvious which jersey certain women are rocking. Other times, not so much. And sometimes, you'll even encounter a Team Scarcity player in sheep's clothing. No matter the case, let's navigate the playing field. Let's assemble your best defense against Team Scarcity to ensure you're focused on your first-draft picks for Team Abundance.

⇒ BIG DEAL DIARY ⇐

Knowing does not equal doing; otherwise, we would all be in perfect health from daily sweating and eating only vegetables. Like fitness influencers (who knew that Photoshop has the same effect as a weeklong broccoli smoothie cleanse?).

This round of diary prompts will guide you toward a significant reduction in "Why them and not me?" moments. Improving this ratio will truly benefit you on all the levels as you spend less time comparing yourself and more time focusing on how you can best improve what you have, so that you can level up how you love, live, and lead.

As you read through the following questions, listen to yourself for the first answers that come to mind for you. Write your answers freely, without judging:

✳ Whom do you feel jealous of in your life, and why do you think you feel jealous of that person? Just be honest; no one will see this but you!

✳ Read what you just wrote previously. Would you categorize it as healthy competition or an unhealthy comparison?

✳ If you said an unhealthy comparison, let's try to go a little deeper to figure out if there is part of your jealousy that we could turn into healthy competition. Please write down one thing you appreciate about this person. Please write down one thing you think this person might appreciate about you.

✳ Do you appreciate that same thing about yourself? Why or why not? Can you sit with something you really appreciate about yourself for a moment? Feel grateful for that one thing you *do* have?

✳ What is one thing you have in common with this person that might help you understand and empathize with him or her a little more?

✳ What is one action you could *stop* doing when it comes to this person? (E.g., going through the person's social media profile, gossiping about the person, being unkind.)

✳ What is one action you could *start* to do when it comes to this person? (Trying bestie blinders, making nice comments on the person's photos, sending the person love and light, etc.)

#BIGDEALBOOK

CHAPTER 6

DRESS UP YOUR BIG DEAL DREAMS

t all started when I bought an overpriced little black dress for a party that I definitely wasn't invited to. And my boyfriend almost dumped me for it. But I'm getting ahead of myself. Let me just drop you right into this scene, mid-shouting match:

"I didn't *lie*!" I sweatily shouted at Hartman. "I dressed up my dreams!" He just looked at me incredulously with his mouth open, not even able to respond to what was, in his opinion, my rapidly elevating level of outright insanity. As I watched him seriously reevaluate his potential future wife, I scrambled to explain: "OK, I know I told you I landed this client before we actually, technically did, but I wasn't lying to you! I was manifesting! It's different!" My brutally honest, Excel-spreadsheet-loving, computer programming, engineer-minded future husband remained firmly unconvinced as he slowly explained, "Erin, there's a hard line between truth and lies."

Before you judge, let me explain . . .

After two "failed" ventures, I just *knew* that my third time at the entrepreneurial bat would be the charm. Why? Well, because I had no other choice. I literally could not afford for it not to be. One day, working from my kitchen table with my "team" (a fresh-out-of-college unpaid intern named Alexa whom I met in the bathroom line of a local dive bar), I realized with horror that I didn't have enough money in my checking account to quickly pay a $100 cell phone bill. Let me just make sure we're clear about this: I had raised seven figures of capital. PMS.com had been covered in *Forbes*. I had worked myself in and then back out of massive debt. And now *I was broke.*

The reality was that after listening to the gurus, taking coffee cup motivational quotes as actual business advice, and hustling my heart out, I was a penniless 31-year-old sitting in my pajamas with my teeth unbrushed at 1 p.m. on a Wednesday. Alexa-the-unpaid-intern absolutely had more money in her checking account than I did at that very moment.

Have you ever experienced a record-scratch life juncture like that? If you have, then you know it triggers a tsunami of desperation that feels like you are drowning on dry land. So you size up this stranger (formerly known as You) and decide she's not who you thought she was. And she's certainly not who you know she is capable of being. As the universe challenged me with a sliming of shame, the bitterness of that instant shocked my mind into seeing right through my carefully curated, fiercely guarded narratives around *why*, at that exact moment, I couldn't pay the most basic of bills.

I was forced to face the chilling reality that maybe it *wasn't* the idea that wasn't good enough. Maybe it *wasn't* that the timing had been wrong. Maybe I had to finally admit that the reason that not one but *two* ventures tanked, and the reason I was broke, the reason I was a failure, was for one reason and one reason only: I simply wasn't enough. I wasn't smart enough. I wasn't good enough. I wasn't strategic and visionary and efficient enough. There was no one and nothing else to point the failure finger at. Falling flat on my face twice was for no other reason than my lack of enoughness. And if you've ever been punched in the face by the invisible enemy of Not Enoughness, you can probably guess what happened next.

After excusing myself from Alexa, I went into my bathroom, locked the door, and bawled on the floor. Afterward, looking in the mirror at my swollen, puffy red face, I gave myself until next month's cell phone bill. If I couldn't pay it, I would quit. It was time to call a spade a spade. Throw in the towel. Wave the white flag. It was just about time to give up on my dreams of being my own boss, and go back to reporting to one that would afford me a steady paycheck in exchange for the shackles of a cubicle. (No shame in a corporate gig by the way, but if that's what I was going to do all along, I should have stayed in that world so I would have a decade of 401(k) investments, savings accounts, and a lot less gray hairs.)

The combination of urgency and desperation to avoid admitting defeat and settling for what I felt was a lose-lose option lit an urgency inside me that I had never experienced. This was like every sports movie of all time when you're down in the fourth quarter and the only option at all is a full-on Hail Mary moment.* And *this* was the moment when Hartman started calling me a liar.

I knew I needed to do two things. First, I had to convince myself (and subsequently the universe) that I was already kind of a Big Deal. This, clearly, was a lie. But here's the thing: I wasn't going into battle with puffy-faced pathetic me. I was going in with Big Deal me, and only she would know *exactly* what type of strategy we needed.

But this attempt at bridging the gap between current Hot Mess me and future Big Deal me was going to require more than a few yoga classes. It was going to require a full system reboot. How? By serving up what can only be described as Big Deal delusion. I wrote the pump-up Post-it® notes (to myself, which I'll tell you more about later) and sent myself motivational text messages. I pretended that I had a huge team and staff catering to my every personal and professional whim. I sent myself actual flowers from a fictional client as a thank you for all the spectacular work we had completed on the client's account. (Oh you think things are getting weird now? Just wait.)

From there, I parlayed my Big Deal delusion into Big Deal action. Naturally, to turn around my small business I would need more than a few small local clients to make ends meet. Being that I was a Big Deal CEO, naturally I only worked with Big Deal clients. Making a list of said Big Deal clients, I wrote out a list of

* If you're not a big sports person, a "Hail Mary" is a long football pass with little chance of completion, typically used when time is running out and no other play is practical. It's an act done in desperation, again with only a very small chance of success.

the most absurd, ridiculous clients I could ever fantasize about landing. Clients that were coveted by some of the biggest, fanciest agencies in the world, from LA to London. Clients that would change the trajectory of my business overnight. Clients that would take us (both Alexa and me) from broke to baller instantly. I couldn't afford slow growth. I couldn't afford to strategically test and learn. I was out of runway. It was now or, as was looking more likely to the point of inevitable, freaking never. Friends, this list was *absurd*. The Olympics. The Super Bowl. And at the very top of that list, the Academy Awards.

I couldn't manifest the whole list, so I just started at the top. I lied to my journal about the productive meeting I'd just had with the Oscars. I lied to my computer and created (but didn't send, obviously) the press release announcing how the Oscars had hired the Socialite Agency. The weirdest thing was I had this mantra the whole time: "The stars will align." I have no idea why—it just came out onto paper one day—so I went with it.

And as the final freaky ultimatum, just to show the universe how serious (desperate) I was, I went to Bloomingdale's and charged an overpriced little black dress to my almost maxed-out credit card. I lied to myself, telling myself this was the dress I was wearing on the red carpet in a few months.

When I told Hartman we had landed the Oscars and we most certainly did not, that's when I crossed the line, and he was technically correct with his categorization. But I knew he was the only one who likely understood my temporary insanity and would forgive me. Or so I hoped. That day when he called me out, I saw the line between lies drawn right there in the sand. (Literally. We were fighting on the beach.) Lie to others *never*.

"Lie" to yourself if you need to (until that lie becomes your new truth, that is).

So what happened next? After that one moment of morally wrong insanity, dressing up my Big Deal dreams (coupled with hard work, a creative idea, and a metric ton of *faith*) began to actually freaking work.

Using what years later became the basis for my "PUB" method (which is outlined in my sales book *Digital Persuasion* and explains that you should open a conversation with something Personal to your recipient, offer something that is truly Useful, and keep it brilliantly Brief), I researched decision makers and reached out to every single Big Deal prospect on my list. Dozens of PUB messages went out into the digital universe. And, of course, no one wrote back. Why would they? I was only a Big Deal in my own mind, and those people were *actually* the Biggest Deals of them all. Except that something peculiar happened. The week my next cell phone bill was due, one of these dozens of Big Deals did write back. An idea I sent to a producer for the Oscars miraculously spawned an email exchange that sparked a live meeting. And I'll never forget sitting in my beat-up Prius (that I had been coasting on the downhills all the way to LA because I was afraid of running out of gas) and crying into a contract. We were hired. By the freaking Oscars.

On the momentous red-carpet day that eventually followed, I remember being backstage with my headset and clipboard managing my newly-hired team of social media journalists when I turned around and found myself face-to-face with Elle freaking Woods. I just stared with my mouth agape, starstruck, as she bounced away with her bubbly laugh. And in that moment, I realized that the stars had literally aligned.

After the event, when I actually sent out my formerly imaginary press release (which you can still find online today), not just my agency but my life was *never* the same. The Oscars led to Fashion Week and Nelson Mandela's family fund-raiser, which led to working with the US Navy in the Pentagon. This one manifestation shot Socialite into the stratosphere, where we had the opportunity to work with some of the world's biggest brands, and I could finally pay for a lot more than just a cell phone bill. I eventually moved into writing books about digital communication (and now audacity!), and now my full-time job is pinch-me incredible. I have the great honor of speaking at conferences around the world helping women and a few good men. I'm living a life that when I think about how far I've come from that horrible phone-bill day, I can cry on demand, I'm so overwhelmed with gratitude.

That's how powerfully you have to believe and desire and work for your vision in order for it to come true. You possess Big Deal Energy that once unlocked, empowers you to behave and operate like the thing you want most in this world has already happened. You audaciously *know* that you *are*, already, a Big Deal and that you deserve this dream. You know in your heart and soul that you radiate that Big Deal Energy, not someday in the foggy future, but right here, right now, exactly where you are. You have to ask yourself: Am I audacious enough to double down on my "delusionially" Big Deal dreams? Am I audacious enough to ignore everyone who calls me crazy? Obviously, your definition of *big* is only for you to define. For me? If at least one person in my inner circle doesn't think I've lost my mind, that's a great indicator that what I'm doing isn't as big as it could be.

You know in your heart and soul that you radiate that Big Deal Energy, not someday in the foggy future, but right here, right now, exactly where you are.

Should you decide those answers are *yes*, can you prepare yourself for the nonsexy fine print that it *is* always darkest before the dawn? Because pushing through with that *one last* effort, that *one last* reinvention, that *one last* message, that *one last* time—that *one last*ness is where the magic almost always happens. "Lying" to yourself (but not others!) about your positive goals, dreams, and desires—even if it's shocking and/or offensive to others or yourself when you admit it—is 100 percent how you can create your own Oscars magic. It's how you can catch your big break to open those big, juicy, legendary opportunities in the movie of your own life. Because it only takes manifesting one dream to trigger the rest into your new reality. It only takes that tipping-point plot twist for your stars to align, just in time.

So let's dive into the *details* of how you can take clear steps toward unlocking your Big Deal Energy and start dressing up your Big Deal dreams, because we all know that attracting begins with action.

POWER UP WITH POST-ITS

Earlier I alluded to my deep love affair with Post-it notes. The variety of colors, the ease with which you can just crumple them and begin again, their ability to live anywhere and stay stuck to anything—I just love them. Virtual presentation? Post-its. Packing list? Post-its.

While I'd always used Post-its for the "to-do"–type items, it wasn't until my friend Judi (yes, the same Judi who called me out on my procrastination back in Chapter 2) shared with me how she would plaster her hotel room with pump-up notes to get psyched before her keynote speeches that I evolved my Post-it usages from the mundane "what to do" into the magical "how to feel." If you're looking for a way to upgrade the efficacy of your positive self-talk, don't underestimate the wizardry of daily self-love notes—*especially* if you are prepping for a Big Deal high-stakes scenario. It sounds a little looney, but I'm obsessed with assembling an army of colorful cheerleaders that can be rooting you on from any room in your home, office, or hotel room! You can be surrounded by good vibes in your bathroom mirror, on your bedside table, or, my personal favorite, when you go to open the fridge. (#SummerIsComing)

But what if you are someone who struggles to actually believe your self-sourced endorsements? I see you because I also struggled with those feelings until I read a study that completely reframed how I leveraged positive self-speak. According to a 2020 edition of *Clinical Psychological Science*, we can optimize the likelihood of our self-talk being more effective if we employ what's been termed "distanced self-talk." Because we tend to believe what others say about us more than what we simply think about ourselves, using our name and speaking in the third person proved to be more powerful in regulating negative emotions. So circling back to promoting yourself to Big Deal status via pink Post-it notes, instead of writing "I am going to rock this meeting!," you would write, "[*insert your name*] is going to rock this meeting!"

Obviously, this can be a slippery slope, as you don't want to descend into scary narcissistic levels of third-person praising in front of others because that would be crossing over from audacious to a-hole. But when it comes to convincing yourself that your BDE is firing and ready for the task at hand, the power of third-person Post-its cannot be underestimated.

BUY YOUR DREAM DRESS

You've heard the old adage that you should dress for the job that you want? Well, the same rule applies when it comes to dressing for the *life* that you want. I believe wholeheartedly that buying my Oscars dress when I had *zero* money to do so was the smoke signal the universe needed to believe just how serious I was about putting an end to my downward spiral and stepping into the success dimension I had been dreaming of. In that delusional power move in the formal dress section of Bloomingdale's, I imagine that swipe of the credit card was the last straw, putting the universe over the edge like *Ugh! Fine! Let's just give it to her already!*

Think of your attire like a military or a sports uniform you want to don before battle. Or the wetsuit you need to go diving. Or the helmet you need to go riding. You simply *suit up* for the success coming your way. And that suit is so much more than physical—it's tricking our minds into believing that we are already living our Big Deal lives for a more frictionless alignment of the natural corresponding Big Deal behaviors, choices, and reactions.

Maybe it's the suit you're rocking for that winning client presentation. Maybe it's the sneakers you're wearing when you accomplish that fitness goal. Maybe it's the bag or wallet you're carrying that the decision maker's business card goes into.

One of the most tangible ways to alert the cosmos/God/angels/the world that you are not here to mess around is to put your money where your mouth is. Or in my case, putting my lack of money where my dreams were.

If you aren't in a position where you can physically purchase something, can you rent or borrow it? Is there a way to equip yourself with a physical representation of the path you are carving, the life you are building, or the outcome you are manifesting? Are you as prepared as possible, with your best foot forward, so that when the universe delivers, you at least look like you were born ready?

I should issue a spoiler alert though: even those that love you the most will likely respond negatively to you in this step of the actualization game. And when (not if) they do, you have two choices. Listen to *them*, lose momentum, and go back to Stuck City. Or listen to *you*, refuse to drink the Haterade, and audaciously stay your course.

Remember: big changes ignite big reactions. Other people's reactions toward you of shock, refusal, or rejection aren't stoplights for you; they're warning lights for them. Warning lights that they should use caution because you're about to make. shit. happen.

WAITING ON WISHES

So let's say you've identified the goals, made the lists, taken the big actions, written the pump up Post-its, visualized the success, ignored the haters, elevated the self-talk, and bought the dress. What's next? You surrender. And you trust. And you wait. But you can be honest with me; maybe you're losing the faith a bit. Where is *he/she/it*? When you find yourself just palms up, waiting for whoever or whatever you believe in to deliver the goods, you might be wondering, "How much longer until this *works*"?

While none of us has a crystal ball, one phenomenon you will notice when you're almost "there" is you'll begin to be generally more passionate or enthusiastic about whatever it is you're chasing down. You might find that you have that "little kid at Christmas" flutter in your heart for no specific reason.

Another element you might note is that suddenly people will mention that "you should" try something or do something, or ask if you have you heard of "xyz"—and it's *scary* close to the exact thing you've been working toward. Other times, you'll hear people talking about what they are working toward, and it's eerily identical to your exact desire.

Maybe you're not experiencing any of this and you're worrying it all will go wrong. Maybe you're feeling anxious about the timing lining up correctly. Maybe you're angry that it hasn't happened sooner because you are "due for it already." Maybe you're a highly practical person like my husband who just doubts that all this "woo-woo hippie stuff" is even real. Maybe you're more of a "prepare for the worst just to be safe" kind of person. Maybe you're getting bogged down by logistics and timelines and details, which I hate to tell ya, are clouding your ability to stay laser-focused on the high-level outcome!

If you've ever experienced a bout of bad luck and said to yourself, *Ugh, I just knew this was going to happen,* that is a big indicator that your emotions are crowding the sacred space needed for your new reality to exist within. Especially if you start to experience fear, worry, anxiety, or doubt after someone else took the winds out of your sails, questioned your sanity, or mocked your dream as being "unrealistic" or "not for you."

So, friend, if you just felt a little too seen in these last few paragraphs, all I can say is watch your words! Be extra intentional and strategic about uttering the most dangerous words out loud like *never*, *hate*, and *can't*! This isn't toxic positivity; these are the laws of the universe. And like the last Indiana Jones movie where it's only until he has the faith to step in the abyss that the bridge beneath his feet is made visible, the same principle applies to you on your quest.

SPREAD THE WORD

This is the most important step of dressing up your dreams, and the one that *so many of us* (hand raises) tend to forget! After you have experienced your "Oscars moment," remember to stop and honor that accomplishment with complete and total gratitude. And I don't mean, "Oh, what a lovely day!" thankfulness. We're talking *radical* gratitude of the highest order. We're talking chills and getting choked up and pinching yourself. Tell all your friends and anyone else who will listen about the unbelievable opportunity that has presented itself to you. Tell strangers in a coffee shop, your neighbors, and, most of all, tell the person in your family or friend group who is least likely to get excited for you. *Tell them all.*

After you have experienced your "Oscars moment," remember to stop and honor that accomplishment with complete and total gratitude.

#BIGDEALBOOK

Like summitting a beautiful hike, sit with your success a minute. Drink in the views and feel the breeze and smell the air. Enjoy that PB&J and watch the birds go by. Marinate in your success for a respectable amount of time to honor what you've just been fortunate enough to witness before you hop on to the next shiny mission. Especially if you are one of those people who just can't help but want to say *yay!* and then quickly move onto the next thing (#guilty). The fastest way I've found to force my soul to savor the moment is to recall in vivid detail a time in my life when not only didn't I have this thing, but when I would have given *anything* to get it. Remember when the *you* from a few weeks or months or years ago would give anything to trade places with the you of today?

So many times, we forget that the situation we find ourselves in right now is one that we would have killed for back in the day.

Also keep in mind that to create the thing/project/place/person you're now enjoying, there are others behind or below or beside you striving with all their might to make it happen. Your hard-won win, for them, is straight up #goals—you are. It's time for a post-accomplishment pat on the back to pay tribute to just how far you've come. Good job you!

So many times, we forget that the situation we find ourselves in today is one that we would have killed for back in the day.

#BIGDEALBOOK

Acknowledge that, yes, the universe delivered, and, yes, you are so thankful, *and* . . . this did not happen by accident. It happened because you made an intentional choice. You wrested back control of your mindset, which is no easy task. You took the terrifying first steps off the ledge and into the darkness without knowing whether or not there would be a bridge, or even a net. You ignored your haters and naysayers. You paid precious attention to your inner GPS lady, and unlike a bad Lyft experience, she did not steer you wrong. You have earned this, you have toiled for this, and you were *destined* to live this dream. Thank yourself, thank everyone who helped get you here, and really savor in the success of this moment for as long as you possibly can. These are the moments that matter. These are the flashes of euphoric joy that will visit you in your last hours. *This* is living a life you love.

When you start to itch to move onto the next thing right away, challenge yourself to stay here now, for a moment longer.

Sear the success into your soul. Feel the joy in your heart. Smile, knowing that whoever or whatever you believe in is always on your side.

⋗ BIG DEAL DIARY ⋖

You don't have to wear a fancy dress for this exercise. Unless you want to, of course.

For these prompts, dig deep and please don't hold back. Radical honesty will set you on your potential path toward realizing those Chanel-and-champagne (or whatever brand and beverage you're into!) dreams that are seeking you just as passionately as you are seeking them. As you read through the following questions, listen to yourself for the first answers that come to mind for you. Write your answers freely, without judging. Which dreams do you want to dress up, attract, manifest into your life? Now review each one and ask yourself how it would *feel* for you and for those around you for this to be your new reality. How will your life change in ways both positive and potentially less than positive?

✳ What do you think is blocking you from this being your reality right now? Is it something out of your control, like the wrong timing, or is it something within your control, like not believing you deserve it?

✳ When you close your eyes, can you *see* the details of this dream? Places, people, smells, colors, sounds?

Can you "experience" what it would be like once it actually happened?

✳ What is one thing you can *do* to begin to put this in motion? Is it to buy the outfit you would wear? Or call someone? Or pull the trigger on the smallest, first decision? What can you put into *action* to move you in the right direction for what it is you seek?

✳ Can you imagine feeling so *grateful* and *thankful* and overwhelmed with the prosperity of accomplishing your biggest desire? Write down exactly what you would do to celebrate successfully making this happen in your life. Be detailed! Not just "Go to dinner," but where? With whom? What do you order? How is the celebratory champagne toast—in your honor— worded? Go down the rabbit hole!

✳ Once you've actualized your Big Deal dream, remember to let your diary know. Cause we're all in this together.

#BIGDEALBOOK

CHAPTER 7

CAPE UP SO YOU DON'T COP OUT

I f you're old enough to have ever dressed up as schoolgirl-era Britney Spears for Halloween, you probably remember what the Yellow Pages were. If not, picture a massive book that included the landline phone number of everyone in your entire city. (Landlines were phones that were connected to walls and incapable of scrolling Instagram.)

Back in the early 2000s, my very first "real-world" job involved combining these relics together to cold-call local Baltimore businesses and ask if they would consider buying local daytime TV advertising airtime. Picture *Anchorman* meets *The Wire*. You know those infomercials that have been mercilessly made fun of on *Saturday Night Live*? Yep, that's what I sold, and most of my exchanges involved getting screamed at and being hung up on.

Now if I've already lost you with all these archaic references, just gather round the TikTok fire and I'll share with thee the tales of old. Our primary tool for selling broadcast ads face-to-face was a printed-out PowerPoint. Said printout was usually tossed directly into the (nonrecycled) trash just after you left the potential client's office. I used this full-color, forest-murdering document to convince clients that it was a good idea to sink thousands of their precious small business dollars into purchasing TV ads on our local broadcast station. (Broadcast is what people used to watch before Hulu and Netflix.)

Ancient business tech education aside, I remember calling my way through the A section of the Yellow Pages on my first day, and after already being reduced to tears less than 20 minutes in, a magical stroke of luck happened—Amos's Amish Market agreed to meet with me. I asked around the office for help, but everyone ignored me—the new rookie kid wearing the sale-rack ill-fitting Express suit. They cackled and teased, "Good luck selling TV ads to an Amish business: they don't even watch TV!" Their big kid bullying stung, and I had the sinking realization that I wasn't going to get any support or guidance.

Suddenly, a Heather Locklear look-alike wearing an immaculate suit walked toward me in slow motion. Pulling down her Dior sunglasses, she gave me a conspiratorial wink. "C'mon girlie. I'll help ya," she offered. Her name was Kim, and I thought she was *the coolest* person I had ever met. (And I still do!) Off we went to Amos's market, and after we sat down next to several Amish women, who were busy deep-frying Oreos, Kim began presenting our PowerPoint to Amos himself—fully bearded, wearing suspenders and straw hat.

Starring in the role of a real-life human clicker, I licked my finger and carefully turned over each PowerPoint page on Kim's nod (slash wink). And as she pitched him, I watched in total and utter awe of her sales superpowers. She acted like every business owner *in the universe* was just dying to advertise on local television. She didn't care what he thought about her fancy sunglasses or her shiny Mercedes parked out front of his establishment that revered nonmaterialistic humility. And just when I thought she couldn't be any more gloriously audacious, she point-blank asked him: "So, Amos, are you ready to put your business on TV or what?"

Fast-forward an hour. As we drove back to the office with a signed contract and a $10,000 deposit check, she revealed to me that it was actually her first week on the job, too. Thank God she was driving because I would have wrecked the car at this revelation. I was *shocked*. Kim didn't care if Amos was offended. Kim didn't care if she got rejected. Kim didn't care if the deep-frying Oreo wives were glaring at her the entire time she was there. She explained her thinking to me, saying, "If you think about it, what was the worst thing that could have happened? He might have said no? So what? We'd grab a few Oreos and move on to the next one!" And with that, she laughed, slid the Diors back on, and cranked up her Outkast CD. *Hey ya!*

Have you ever witnessed real-life superpowers in action and just wondered to yourself, *How did she do that?* That was totally me the whole ride back to the city that day. I couldn't stop drilling Kim with questions about her savvy sales prowess: "How did you make that deal happen? Have you always known how to sell? How can I do what you just did? How are you not nervous?

As she shared her backstory, I learned that she had been hustling her entire life. She explained it to me like this: "Erin, either you have the skills or you need to borrow someone else's until you do. It's like acting. Just use mine till you get there." Done and *done*.

The next day, as I picked up the phone to begin another day full of rejection, to eradicate that pit in my stomach of fear and anxiety, I just imagined what Kim would say or do with each phone call. Well, she would get in character. How would she do that? Well, she'd wear a costume. So in a dusty old basement conference room with one of those Star Trekky telecoms, I slid on a pair of sunglasses (Target, not Dior), and something truly magical happened as I started to dial through the B section of the Yellow Pages. The negative reactions, hang-ups from annoyed people, and plain old *rejection* suddenly didn't sting quite so much.

With each brush-off, I found myself taking it less and less seriously and looking at it more like a game. Wait: Was I actually having *fun* getting shot down by strangers dozens of times? Cloaked in Kim's audacity cape, I was still me—but a grittier, wittier, more fearless me. I felt like I suddenly possessed a skill, a superpower that I didn't really have . . . or did I?

A year later, after smiling and dialing in that dusty old basement borrowing Kim's sales superpowers, she was ranked number 1 in the nation out of 35 different local stations, but I was hot on her heels at number 2—with my very own pair of Dior sunglasses. And let's just say the other salespeople weren't laughing at me anymore—especially when Amos decided to renew his contract.

Contrary to today's advice (particularly in professional settings) about specialization being spectacular, you and I know (and Kim's résumé was a shining example) that killing it in life isn't really about discovering your *one* superpower or your *one* strength. That's a lot of pressure and feels very limiting, doesn't it?

The truth is, and we all know this to be true: different scenarios demand different superpowers. And whether you are struggling to secure more personal strength when it comes to sales, negotiation, healthier relationships, or a more resilient mindset —no matter what obstacle you're up against, there is a superpower you can tap into to help you master the moment.

The truth is, and we all know this to be true: different scenarios demand different superpowers.

#BIGDEALBOOK

When do you know it's time to call in superpower skill support? Here's how: Take your last challenging moment, the tough crowd, the tanking meeting, the digital rejection, the awkward date, whatever. When you pause to reset in those sticky situations, you'll probably experience one of three immediate reactions:

1. *I 100 percent am going to be able to turn this thing around—this isn't my first rodeo.*

2. *I might have this, but I'm not really sure, so fingers crossed!*

3. *This plane is going down in flames, I do not have control of this aircraft, and I need mayday support ASAP!*

This chapter is about what to do when your reaction is #2 or #3, where you can rescue your mission from going south by "borrowing" someone else's piloting abilities. When you find yourself struggling to master the moment, operate efficiently, or communicate clearly, you can take Kim's advice and borrow someone else's skill set for those junctures where it feels too challenging or impossible to execute all on your own. Because after all, a superpower is just a skill with a cape.

Let's take Kim's "superpower," aka audacious skill, of being an incredible sales professional as an example. Have you ever had to reach out to someone you didn't know and ask the person to buy something from you? Or sign a petition? Or donate money to a cause? Or maybe you found yourself in a situation where you were at the mercy of strangers if you lost your phone and needed to get directions or call someone? It is one of the scariest scenarios to put yourself in because the likelihood of getting shot down is *high*. It is terrifying to voluntarily put yourself in a scenario where rejection is really likely. But some people are impervious to the cringey feelings of rejection. Some people are born better at sales than others. Of course, you can learn, study, practice, put in the reps . . . but what if in the meantime you could borrow someone else's superpower, just until you logged enough reps to cultivate your own?

If you find yourself in a situation that you're shrinking away from, feeling underprepared for, or just straight up don't feel like you have what it takes to triumph, you can activate your Big Deal Energy by swapping out the old "fake it till you make it" for a little "cape up so you don't cop out." For those occasions where you just don't feel like you have what it takes to "fake" it from your own arsenal, what if you simply channeled someone else's talents or courage or bold, IDGAFness? Just like wearing some-one else's hat or dress (or sunglasses), donning this mental cape means you're still operating as you, but just accessorizing your persona with someone else's super-skills. (Not forever—just until you develop your own.) Like I did with Too Tan Todd in that tampon-tossing boardroom and after I learned to let rejection roll off my back from Kim, I was still showing up as me; I was just renting their radness. I channeled their confidence to better navigate the negativity of the moment.

Don't be afraid to "rent" someone else's radness until you discover and develop your own.

#BIGDEALBOOK

The beauty of this sassy strategy is that it begins to com-pound its efficacy the more you exercise it. Every time you inten-tionally cape up to rise above everyday mini-moments, you'll start to watch as your audacity accessorizes your emotional out-fits in progressively higher-stakes scenarios. Is there a sweaty situation that you're facing right now? Maybe it's an ask or a decision or a deletion, where swinging someone else's skill set over your hypothetical shoulders might take you from an awk-ward entrance to a fabulous one.

Now before we go any further down this controversial cape path, I can hear what some of you are defiantly declaring: *What? No. No, no, no, Erin. I'm not going to not be myself. I'm not going to just chameleon my way through, pretending to be some-*

one I'm not! I left that garbage back in middle school where it belongs. I stand for authenticity! Just be yourself, no matter what! OK. OK; me, too! Yes to everything you just thought . . . *and* I'm not suggesting that you don't be yourself. I'm merely suggesting that when you're facing down your next super-scary, seriously sweaty scenario, you temporarily "borrow" a specific, custom superpower from someone who you know would inherently rock this moment in a way you just don't feel particularly ready or equipped to do with the same success rate. Think of caping up as being yourself—but optimizing your awesome by borrowing a boost of bodaciousness.

When you find yourself in one of life's paramount positions that make your heart beat out of your chest and your palms sweat more than a sixth grader during a slow, couple's skate song, it's a relief to know you can rely on this Advil-like accessory. Because, remember, a real-life superpower is not gifted from a mysterious planet called Krypton; it's just a skill with a cape. And whether you're struggling to secure more superhero-level strength when it comes to your finances, your health, your relationships, your mindset, no matter what season you are weathering right now, there is an audacity cape hanging in your closet of consciousness that is dry-cleaned and ready for its big debut.

THREE LITTLE CAPES: A CAPE FOR EVERY CONUNDRUM

Welcome to Boldstrom. I'm Erin, and I'll be your personal audacity shopper today. It looks like you're shopping for a scenario that could use a little extra Big Deal Energy? Lucky for you, this season we're featuring three superpowered styles. No matter which cape feels the most "you" for your moment, each option is fully equipped to send you flying up and up and away past naysayers and competitors.

Here's how it works. Let's say you find yourself in a bit of a prickly plight where you know you need to turn up your audacity a notch, but like setting the volume of your iPhone when you're the hostess of the cocktail party, maybe you're unsure what the perfect volume should be. Are people ready to turn it up and dance till the wee hours? Or is your event shaping up to be more of an intimate smattering of one-on-one deep dialogues? Or maybe instead, you find yourself on someone else's turf, terrified of being judged, rejected, or simply disliked! Maybe, because underneath all your awesome, you're just having an off day where your humor is falling flat, your sarcasm is misunderstood, or your usual brilliance is missing the mark. If you said *yes* to any of the above, here's a super-simple three-step formula to snap you out of your suckiness:

- **Step 1:** Evaluate the scene and ask yourself which brand of cape would best propel you toward phenomenal: the Seeker, the Warrior, or the Creator? Do you need to discover a new direction? Defend a nonnegotiable? Create a new option? (More on all three of these in just a minute.)

- **Step 2:** After you've diagnosed your dilemma, call to mind the first person, dead or alive, who you know personally or not, that would know *exactly* what to do in this situation. Who do you know that would navigate these choppy waters with smashing success? PS: Just like in the old days of academia, trust your first answer here.

- **Step 3:** Mentally rent the runway of radical. Cape up and cloak yourself in someone else's superpower. And with your borrowed audacity, you *find the thing* (Seeker), you *fight the thing* (Warrior), or you *make the thing* (Creator).

Let's back it up for a second to step 1—cape selection and break down each cape.

Cape 1: The Seeker

The Seeker is the cape you want if you hear yourself saying, "I just wish I could find a new . . . xyz."

Whether you're in need of a new job, a new strategy, a new relationship, a new direction, a new place, or even just a new mindset, the Seeker is for when you're faced with finding that new option! The superhero whose cape you're looking to borrow in this instance is the dynamo in your life who refuses to settle for what currently *is*. It's the gal you know who is consistently audacious enough to look for (and find!) more fitting options to optimize the opportunity—everyone else's opinions be damned.

For me, that's Cara O'Connor. (Remember Cara from back in Chapter 1 who traded makeup for medicine?) Whenever I'm secretly dragging my feet on pulling the trigger because deep down I'm petrified of what people will say or think when I make a wild U-turn, I cape up with Cara's audacity, go with my gut, and pursue what it is I'm looking for with Big Deal Energy. Who is your Cara O'Connor? And if no one comes to mine, Cara O'Connor can be your Cara O'Connor! What if you caped up with her audacity *just* until you own your own? I dare you to try. (And please message me on Instagram @mrs.erin.king when you do so I can hear what happened!)

Cape 2: The Warrior

Perhaps the most audacious of the capes is the Warrior cape. This is the cape for you if you've ever found yourself in a situation that calls for audacity in defending something bigger than yourself. When you must defend what is right. When you must oppose what is unjust. When you must fight to get the *thing* changed, implemented, funded, or approved. This is for the times when an individual or an institution has crossed one of your nonnegotiable lines in regard to values. This is the cape that sometimes moves you from just channeling superpowers to operating audaciously as a real-life superhero.

Now rocking the Warrior cape might literally mean engaging in a legal battle or a protest march to right a wrong. It might mean reporting something to the appropriate authorities. It might mean being transparent about someone when confronted by a parent or boss. It might mean digging deep beyond your hesitation to share where you really stand on a political or cultural issue to your social media network, even in spite of potential (probable) digital backlash. And if there is someone in your life whose superpower is one of those, then there you go: you know what to do.

One of my dearest friends (let's call her Sara) works for an old-school pharmaceutical company headquartered in a very traditional part of the country. Let's just say the C-level at this organization is still jam packed with a bunch of old-school white dudes. Sara is smart as a whip, has a phenomenal personality, and has that ability to make anyone fall in love with her within minutes of meeting. No one is impervious to her Midwestern-farm charm because it's so darn genuine. So as a sales rep, Sara won so many president's club awards that the company had no choice but to promote her to be the highest-ranking female manager, just one step under the all-male executive leadership team.

One of the guys Sara reported to, Jack, was so flirtatious with some of the much lower-ranking female employees that a handful of them—right hand to God—called him "Big Daddy." No, this is not an episode of *Mad Men*, and, yes, unfortunately, in many organizations, this crap is still alive and well. So I bet you can guess where this story is heading.

One day, at a team happy hour, Jack said to Sara (and I know this sounds like something out of a movie, but I swear on my mother), "I'm a married man, but working with someone as beautiful as you is going to be tough." Sara was stunned—and nauseated. After she clearly rejected his advances, he began to make her life a total nightmare. He interrupted her in meetings, undermined her authority to her team, and micromanaged her so he could purposely waste her precious time to the point of sabotage. He even reassigned her to manage the lowest-performing sales team in the country: the team in thirty-fourth place.

Now I can hear you yelling just like I did, "He can't do this! You have to go to HR! Report him! Get this sleazebag fired!" So why didn't she report his actions?

Well, according to Sara, at this company, all the C-level guys have known each other since college. And when similar scenarios like this happened in the past (one had happened to a female coworker as recently as a few months prior), they would fire the person reporting the harassment, tell everyone at the company a different narrative, and bury the victim in legal fees until she went away. They would then call all their other "boys' club" executive buddies around the industry to warn them about the candidate, ensuring that person wouldn't make it to any final-round interviews.

Now please hear me on this: I'm not saying that if you find yourself in a similar situation to Sara's that you don't immediately report anything illegal to the proper people. For the vast majority of organizations, that is 100 percent the smart move. And in most organizations, you will be protected and the harasser will be punished accordingly. But Sara was working for an outlier of a company. So instead of feeling like a victim and taking the risk of outsourcing her battle to an untrustworthy process, she decided to take matters into her own hands. She really wanted to fight the screwed-up system in a way that would win. She didn't only want to win her individual battle: she wanted to win the war for the women who would come after her.

So Sara got to work. First, she devoured every book on management strategies that she could get her hands on. Then she began slowly firing her underperforming team one by one and replacing them with her own candidates. This was deeply shocking and offensive in a company where 90 percent of the workforce are lifers—including the managers who had hired the slackers from the thirty-fourth-place team. Let's just say the executive leaders weren't a fan of this move. She then worked with individual team members, one on one, and taught each *exactly* how she had won so many president's club awards. She used her own money to create additional incentives outside of what was technically offered by the company. Again, this was frowned upon. She spent all day, every day, hand-holding and molding each team member, guiding her team toward greatness. She gave up her weekends, her nights, and pretty much her entire social life for 18 months with one goal in mind: to fight her way to number one.

She ignored Jack's attempts at sabotaging her, she ignored the leadership team doubting her methods and questioning her management style, and she worked with one hell of an audacious attitude. Because when you're a woman with something to prove in a legacy corporate setting like that, oftentimes a heavy dose of shock and awe is the only way to truly make shit happen.

Within 18 months, Sara shocked the entire organization when her team's name was called at the annual sales meeting. They finished not in the top 10, or the top 5—which would have been unbelievable—but in first place. I remember her sending me the dark grainy video someone had taken at the reception, and my watching it with tears pouring out of my eyes and a big smile on my face as I saw Jack forced to award her the highest accolade in the company—a dramatic, inspiring, complete turn-around success story in front of the entire C-level and the rest of the organization. I still get chills thinking about the look on her face, and the look on his as he shook her hand in defeat.

Fast-forward to today, and Sara is still the company record holder of the number one team manager, for four years in a row. So when someone from Sara's team shared how Jack had hit on her, Sara now knew she had the clout and the ammo she needed. She just needed her army. So she quietly asked around if anyone else had had a negative experience with Jack, and sure enough, several more women stepped forward.

When she went to HR with her influence and her proof, the company fired its first C-level executive for inappropriate behavior for the first time in the company's history. New training and policies were implemented to prevent and report future harassment for women at the company going forward. And guess who was offered apologies and Jack's job? Yep. Sara. But, of course, by then she was rocketing off to a new opportunity. To win a new battle. Like an audacious Warrior woman does.

Whenever I think about fighting for what I believe in and I feel nervous about people's reactions or the potential obstacles, I channel my inner Sara and don my Warrior cape.

Who is your Sara? Who is the person in your life who has the grit, the determination, the strategy to fight for what's right, the Big Deal Energy to ignore the pushback—and win? Or maybe, you found yourself retweeting Sara's every move. Maybe it reminded you of an eerily similar circumstance that you managed to rise above in your past. If so, it's my hope that you will share your grit and determination with the women in your world—and that you will have the audacity to be someone else's Sara.

Cape 3: The Creator

Lastly, the Creator is your cape if you hear yourself saying, "I just need to find a way to *create* xyz." You'll find yourself in this situation often if you're an entrepreneur, artist, writer, musician, engineer, teacher, coach, or leader of a small team. Or even if you're someone who lives for a good make-your-own-sundae bar. Or if you find yourself in a slightly less enjoyable scenario like, say, being alive during a global pandemic.

This particular cape has been a wardrobe staple during the pandemic (or as I like to call it, the Poundemic). But I'm getting ahead of myself; let's back up a sec.

When COVID-19 hit, my full-time job as a keynote speaker at packed, live convention centers came to a screeching halt—like millions of others in the live events business. Dozens of events were canceled or postponed until further notice, and thousands of dollars were lost. Some events went virtual, but many just kicked the can down the road, rescheduling over and over again. Maybe you also had to experience the surreal devastation of watching a business or venture you'd worked your butt off to build for years all but vanish within a matter of weeks.

After I reacquainted myself with the unmatched comfort of constant white carbohydrates while binge-watching everything I could find, from *Downton Abbey* to *Gossip Girl*, a moment of temporary insanity descended upon me, and I ambitiously went to trade my sweatpants for jeans.

In that moment, I knew it was time to stop eating pizza and start figuring out how to pay bills again. But I felt more stuck than my damn zipper and infinitely more disappointed. After spending the last 15-plus years starting three organizations from scratch, riding the roller coaster of wins and losses, feasts and famines, I'd finally gained traction with a business that I truly loved. And it was looking like I had to reinvent—*again*. Sigh.

It felt insurmountable, overwhelming, and for the first time since my teens, I found myself battling legitimate depression. I started having weird dreams, hopeless thoughts, and I withdrew from my friends both online and offline. I started drinking heavily to escape and adopted this kind of "pretend laugh" with others because I didn't feel any actual joy. One particularly dark day, I was sitting at my desk, sad and desperate to feel even a flicker of motivation or hope, so I sent a fake-cheerful email to my community for the first time in months as a last-ditch effort to snap me out of my "poor me" paralysis.

And as I did, my phone notifications went crazy as 412 autoresponder emails bounced back. Confused, I started reading through each message: "Furloughed." "Fired." "Leave of absence." "On hold for the foreseeable future." I felt a lump in my throat as it dawned on me that hundreds of friends, clients, colleagues in the event industry, and so many more were dealing with catastrophic levels of challenge. As I read each familiar name, I snapped out of my self-pity party and realized how much of a jerk I was being. How dare I be so self-absorbed to forget that this was a collective, universal, human experience? That these stats scrolling across the television night after night were not nameless, faceless strangers somewhere far away, but my direct colleagues and clients!

And just when I felt the darkness pushing me even deeper under the surface of sadness for the state of the world, little life preservers began to pop up in my inbox. I saw emails announcing new ventures and concepts. A local 55-year-old restaurant owner we knew from Laguna was learning how to do delivery using an app for the first time ever. A 67-year-old local jewelry maker from back East was learning how to put photos of her treasures on Facebook marketplace. A trade-show booth-builder I'd known from my days working with exhibitors had set up his own custom shop in his garage to make patio furniture. One of my girlfriends who was a schoolteacher had created Zoom groups for overwhelmed homeschooling parents to brainstorm success strategies (and commiserate a little, of course).

As I read these digital deliveries of grit, sheer scrappiness, and old-fashioned *can-do* attitudes, I got chills. For the first time in a long time, I knew it was time to quit the crying. And stop the emotional eating. And cancel my Netflix account. Without really thinking about it, I wrote down each Creator's name on a Post-it® and slapped the notes to the wall behind my computer. And every time I found myself sliding back down into taking up residence at Poor Me Place, I looked at those names. I borrowed their truly inspiring audacity when I didn't have any of my own left. I caped up so I didn't cop out.

I borrowed their truly inspiring audacity when I didn't have any of my own left. I caped up so I didn't cop out.

#BIGDEALBOOK

I channeled their creative spirits to inspire my own efforts to create my way out of despair and into another new business. I learned video production (alongside my husband), and we started shooting highly produced creative virtual keynotes from the mountains and the beaches. I launched my online course "The Social Media Spa," which now has thousands of network marketers taking a "spa day" to improve their social selling. I created a new podcast, website, and email newsletter. And rather than spending a fortune on outsourcing the work, I learned how to design, code, and edit, and not by going back to school but by YouTubing it. I YouTubed my way through every single mind-numbingly detailed tutorial out there, pausing each video about every three seconds as I painstakingly tried not to get lost with each new step. It sucked. It was brutal. But, remember, when *you* work, your plan does too. Remembering that if these Creators had the audacity to reinvent, then so could I. For the first time since I started my career, I started observing my industry, my DMs, and even my Netflix queue (*Social Dilemma*, anyone?) through a brand-new lens.

After one night of serious contemplation about social media's impact on our lives beyond business (what I had preached, taught, and written about for almost a decade), I decided to pivot my business from digital communication and move into a brand-new space: helping women become more audacious. I wrote this book with the highest of hopes to do exactly that. Borrowing the audacity of these Seekers, Warriors, and Creators, I created my way out of my depression and into reinventing my entire business—just like they had. I even started mountain biking since my beloved Orangetheory Fitness is still closed, and after three months of what felt like zero progress, my jeans finally started to zip. (Just barely, and with shallow breathing, but still! Small wins are big wins!)

What if *you* reframed the way you absorb the actions of those around you and instead of feeling despairing or sad, you borrowed their creative fuel to help relight your fire? If you know people who have managed to keep their business not just surviving but thriving—can you ask them how they did it? If you're finding that your business or your job is suddenly less relevant in the face of changing marketplaces and trends, can you seek out someone in an industry that is similar to yours and explore pivoting your business that way? If you're feeling uninspired to keep going, can you FaceTime one of those friends who looks like they have it all together, have a few laughs, and make a few deposits into your positivity bucket?

Maybe you're reading this thinking, *Well, goooood for you, Erin; so thrilled for you that you have so many sassy sisters and local hustlers to tap into.* Fair enough, and I hear you. Keep in mind that it's OK if you don't have capes to borrow yet. Who are the people you follow on social media that are crushing it right now? Just because you don't know them in real life, that doesn't mean you can't message them and ask how they managed to power through the "corona coaster." Ask them about their morning routine, what they're reading, or whether or not they have a morning mantra. Because if it's working for them, then why can't it work for you?

If you feel awkward randomly reaching out to someone you don't know directly, why not download a few podcasts from your favorite authors or personalities? (I hear *Highlights with Erin King* is pretty legit.) Can you run a search for female entrepreneurial associations, groups, or even meetups to help you cultivate some new capes to borrow? Are there any books you've been thinking about buying from kick-ass women but never actually press the "complete purchase" button? It just takes some curiosity and connecting to begin to multiply your motivational relationships, even if they are just one way—which is always better than no way. So go ahead and start finding your sources of inspiration wherever you can find them and create your way out of the darkness. You have what it takes to create with intention so you're propelled towards the light.

SELECTING YOUR SUPER-SQUAD

Speaking of motivational relationships, let's download about those all-elusive #squadgoals. Whether you're talking about sports, sorority sisters, or your business team—you know that a super-squad is born when you manage to merge just the right motley crew of skills together. Sure, the stakes are high when it's Q4 crunch time at your company or when you're playing a championship lacrosse game, but they're infinitely *higher* when we're talking about something more life and death. Specifically, *your* life. So what does a championship roster of Team Abundance players look like? Well, it typically consists of your offensive players, your defensive players, and your sideline cheer squad. (If you hate sports analogies and sports and all things "team talk"—maybe swap it for the setup of your favorite reality show. Picture one of those baking shows, and your squad is made up of every individual who can nail a multilayered art deco cake with synchronized, time-limited *precision*.)

First, your offensive players are the women in your life who help put points on the board for you. Professionally, this is the gal who helps you negotiate a higher salary or advocate for your promotion. She is the one who has the ear of the one who matters in order to get your proposal green-lighted by the board. Personally, this is the girlfriend you need who takes charge when you had the fight or the breakup or you're lost in life. She plans the night (the girls' weekend, the new hobby, etc.), brings the wine, and outlines the plan. She picks you up and handles things when you just don't have the reserves to do it yourself. When she bosses you around, in that lowest of the low moment, it truly feels like a blessing. She is your fieriest friend who has more than a few ideas on exactly what it is you should do.

She's a super-clutch gal to have on your team, but maybe you're wondering how does one recruit more of these bold babes? Easy. Start speaking up and telling other women how much they rock. How? Get better at friend flirting. What's friend flirting? It's when you vocalize a genuine admiration for another woman's kick-ass qualities in way that's both engaging and disarming. And when you level up your friend flirting, you can expect to see the door to more meaningful conversations and relationships swing wide open over time. If your squad has been a little lacking lately for whatever reason, friend flirting is a must-master. Personally, you'll expedite new friendships in pretty much any cocktail party or airport lounge. Professionally, you'll experience the functionality of friend flirting in two key areas: one, *your productivity* in terms of how you connect with your peers and, two, *your advancement trajectory* when it comes to women you're reporting to. Just like in the animal kingdom montage from *Mean Girls*, it's critical that you immediately telegraph *friend* not foe as fast and as honestly as possible from your very first interaction. Think of it like survival of the flirtiest. But be warned: you should *never* try to fake it, because like animals we can smell that shit a mile away.

I remember when one of my Socialite employees was really struggling to connect with her all-female team. No one was cooperating with her, they were withholding resources, and a few times they even left her off a meeting invite she should have definitely been included on. Besides being frustrating and hurtful, it was seriously impacting her performance. One day she came to me in tears and asked, "What am I doing wrong?" I explained to her that she needed to show the people on her team that she truly cared about them on a more personal level. She responded and explained that she wasn't here to make friends; she just wanted to come to work, do her job, and go home. While I applauded her commitment to work, I explained that without cultivating those personal relationships, her professional success would only continue to suffer. I encouraged her to tell me what she really liked or admired about her closest coworkers; her answer: "I don't know. I've never really thought about it." And in that moment, she finally saw the root cause of her problem, and to her credit, she vowed to do better.

The next day, she complimented one of our project managers on the pasta creation she whipped up on Instagram the night before (to which the manager responded, in shock, "I didn't even know you followed me"). Another day, she left a little bag of dog treats on one of her designer's desks because she saw her bring her pup to work often. And, slowly, she delivered honest compliments around ideas, social media shares, and more during the weeks that followed. Over time different members of the team evolved into champions for her, retweeting her ideas in client meetings and advocating for her concepts in brainstorm sessions. *That* is the raw power of giving sincere compliments and, even more importantly, caring about others.

Not only is recruiting more offensive players to your team is the most efficient way to put points on the board, but those relationships oftentimes turn out to be some of the most vital in your personal life as well.

Team Abundance also needs defense players. Your defensive players are your protectors. Professionally, they are the ones who back you when you're under attack. When your ideas, strategy, or proposal is under fire. They defend you to coworkers who wish you ill. They stand up for your ideas when someone questions them unnecessarily. Personally, they are the ones who call out anyone treating you like garbage. They bring to your attention anyone who isn't being a respectful superfan. They are the ones who will not tolerate negative self-talk. These are the friends who tell you to sue the people that cross you. They are your defenders.

Most of us would probably agree that since defense wins championships, we could definitely use some extra defenders on our squad, but how do you discover such dynamos? If you're having a hard time recruiting a stronger defense, your best bet is to defend *first*. Stand up for her in a meeting. Stick by her when times get hard. Speak up for her when she's not in the room. Start by being the friend you want in your corner when the chips are down.

To round out the squad, you have your sideline sisters. Your cheer squad gals. These are your lovebug buddies who may not coach you on the way forward or defend you against the enemy, but they love the hell out of you and will cheer you on until they're hoarse. This squad includes women like your mom or a similar mother figure who may be clueless about what you should do at work but is always sending you "Atta girl" texts anyway. These supporters will listen to you rant, ramble, and cry about things they may not fully understand or have experience with. This group could also be the friends from high school or college who have known you for so long and even though your lives are vastly different, and you have less in common than you used to, they send the cards, make the calls, donate to the cause, follow the account, like the posts, and buy your thing. They may not always get it, but they love you for it anyway.

I cannot emphasize strongly enough how vital it is to prioritize nurturing and resuscitating your cheer squad sisters.

So where exactly does one recruit these three different types of Team Abundance players? How can you get started building your even more badass bench? Your opportunities are endless. First, say yes to invites. You won't need to do this forever, but if you're realizing your bench is light and you're shifting into proactive squad recruitment mode, it will assist tremendously. Second, ask personal questions and remember their answers for the next time you see them to follow up. Not like TMI personal, but questions like "How did you meet your significant other?" or "Where did you grow up?" Third, ask super-connectors for solution-focused introductions. You know those gals who feel like micro-influencers (they work in PR, networking marketing, fitness, etc.) and who maintain a broad circle? Ask them if they know someone who can help you with your design challenge, or with picking the right restaurant for a birthday celebration, or even just someone who has the best recommendations or expertise when it comes to parenting, creativity, research, or whatever you enjoy doing or find challenging. Finally, put reminders on your calendar to get together with one new person a week, whether that's meeting for brunch, attending a concert, going for a walk, or even doing a "get to know you" Zoom for 30 minutes. The idea here is to be intentional around engineering potential friend-making moments, and not just leave it up to serendipity.

If you already have a cheer squad of people you *love*, I'm *so* happy you found them. And I need you to hear me on this: when the mythical empty Saturday afternoon happens and you have time to kill, call them for a 10-minute "You crossed my mind, and even though I have to go soon, I love you" chat. This may not feel like enough to maintain these relationships, but it's better than zero. Treasure your old relationships, even if sometimes it feels like you and they are existing in different dimensions of life. These friendships take so little to respark and yet are the most worth it because these friends have known you, loved you, and been cheering you on through all your seasons, from winning to losing to everything in between. Will you call them for me today? Please?

The truth about achieving Big Deal success is this: it's *possible* but highly unlikely you'll get there on your own. Build your squad, find your people, and friend-flirt—then you can sit back and watch as those transformative relationship results ignite the most unimaginable of opportunities.

⇉ BIG DEAL DIARY ⇇

Let's put in some reps together and activate our Seekers, our Creators, and/or our Warriors. Remember, the goal of caping up is not to pretend to be someone you're not for the rest of your life. It *is*, however, a highly effective superpower transition plan to support and bring out your own latent superpowers. You're just borrowing the mantle while yours is in the shop being bedazzled. So the next time you find yourself in a situation where you don't feel ready to rock it, you borrow the mindset, the attitude, or the experience or the energy of someone who does. Eventually, either it rubs off on you, or it helps you figure out how to activate your own superpower. It's just a little trick to bridge the gap between where you are today and where you've decided you want to be in the not-so-distant future. And the fastest way to go from borrowing to owning can be found by completing the following questions as authentically as possible:

✳ Which of these sentences would be the easiest one (or the first one you gravitate toward) for you to fill in the blank? It's also OK if you want to fill out all of them, but pay attention to the one that was easiest for you to answer first.

    ๑ I just wish I could *find* a new

    _____.

ᕲ I must fight

_____.

ᕲ I just need to find a way to *create*

_____.

✳ Look at the cape you homed in on first. Who are the people in your life, living or dead, whom you know personally or don't, that you feel would best be equipped to successfully navigate that type of situation? You can list as many as come to mind. If you don't know, you can describe what that type of person would be like. What qualities would that person have?

✳ What situation(s) are you feeling ill-equipped to handle right now? Like you don't have the right skill set, or you feel you're in over your head, or you just feel paralyzed in place?

✳ What is one action you could take to show up more audaciously in this situation? How could you navigate it more toward the outcome that you want? What would you tell yourself to mentally "cape up" to come out the other side of this with the result you're looking for?

✳ If you agree to promise yourself that the next time you are in this scenario, you will cape up and act audaciously, please write the following: "I'm cloaked in what it takes to show up powerfully in this situation."

(And please read that sentence out loud. At least three times. As many times as you need to.)

As a close to each of these journaling exercises, we're going to practice what we discussed in the introduction— call it a mantra, if you will. Remember when I had you say out loud, "I'm kind of a Big Deal?" Did you manage to say it boldly, or did you feel as ridiculous as an old millennial making TikTok dance videos? (Maybe that's just me.)

Well, I want you to try it again now. Because you do know how to dance. And the nineties are back anyway. So adjust your scrunchie, fix your fanny pack, and say it with me: *"I'm kind of a Big Deal."*

#BIGDEALBOOK

CHAPTER 8

PREP FOR THE PARADOX

"**A**ny healthy, married woman who voluntarily chooses not to have children is just selfish."

I can still remember the sting of my mother's words as if I had swum face first into an angry jellyfish. After months of avoiding the topic, I had finally admitted that Hartman and I had decided to live our lives child-free, by choice. Stuttering, with my heart beating out of my chest, I reminded her of our expanding clan of nieces, nephews, godchildren, and sweet second cousins up and down the East Coast, from the Irish Gargans of Boston to the Southern Faulkners of Charlotte. I reminded her how much I had cherished my big sister role helping her and my dad raise my 11-years-younger sister and fast-forward to today how we were so grateful and blessed in our equally cherished roles as Uncle H and Auntie E.

But trying to explain the idea of a voluntarily child-free life to a Catholic woman whose father was the youngest of nine children on a farm in Ireland and who quit working on her master's degree and gave up a career she loved in her twenties to dedicate her life to raising three children was like trying to explain the wonders of veganism to a lifelong cattle farmer. My mother, in her prime mom years, was a *force*. She didn't take any medication during childbirth because she didn't want to expose us to anything that could be toxic. Long before Whole Foods was a thing, she was blending vegetables to make her own organic baby food. She had memorized her copy of *Parenting the Strong-Willed Child* front to back. Her flashcard dedication was so fierce (the story goes) that apparently one of my aunts left after one babysitting night highly distressed that her own children might be developmentally challenged after hearing my brother and I spelling out words with more than one syllable. (That edge evaporated by kindergarten, but still, for a hot sec, apparently we were preschool prodigies.) My mom was a *magnificent* mom, and I'm so thankful I won the mom lottery and got her. *And . . .*

She never came out and said this directly, but when it came to procreation, the implication was something along the lines of this: How could I not play by the rules? She fulfilled her maternal destiny, and now it was time for me to pick up the parental poopy diaper torch and do the same. My mom was ready to cash in her hard-earned supermom chips. Her reward? A few more grandkids. Over the course of fragmented awkward conversations here and there, I could feel my sweet parents looking at me with thinly veiled horror: How dare I renege on my responsibilities as a living, breathing uterus? Or as my dad incredulously asked one time, "Did I hate children or something?"

When my mom is distressed, she gets what I call "sad mad." She wants to cry, but crying is for wimps, so she speaks in this scary stern voice from her teaching days that is truly terror inducing. And as her sad mad began to build, my inner good girl desperately banged on the door and begged to be let out. It didn't matter that I was a married grown-ass woman in my mid-thirties, I still felt that good-girl pleading voice pulling at my heart: "Please! We can change our minds! Maybe you're wrong about how you feel! Everyone does it! What's wrong with you? It's not too late! Do you really want to let down the people who dedicated their lives to raising you, you selfish millennial?" It's precisely moments like this that we fear so much, where we're ready to betray ourselves. See, the scariest part of ghosting your inner good girl is taking the risk that you might be ghosted in return by whoever it is you're failing to please. And in that awful hour, you need your audacity the most.

The scariest part of ghosting your inner good girl is taking the risk that you might be ghosted in return by whoever it is you're failing to please. And in that awful hour, you need your audacity the most.

#BIGDEALBOOK

Taking a deep breath, I borrowed the Warrior cape. Wrapped in my borrowed IDGAFness, I glared and shushed and turned my back on the scared former good girl in trouble with her momma. If you've ever pushed through your fear of standing by your decision when someone you love (or admire and respect in the case of a work scenario) is highly disappointed in it, you know it straight-up sucks at the highest level of suckage. But when it's your life and your choices and the stakes are highest, when you find yourself sitting at that critical intersection, your Big Deal self really doesn't have any other choice but to trust that your inner GPS lady knows *your* way.

Maybe, as in my case, you're battling an archaic cultural contract that you never signed off on in the first place. Maybe you're fighting for the freedom to make a monumental decision about your own body and your own life. Maybe you're warring against thousands of years of tradition declaring what your purpose as a married, unmarried, or "none of your business what my marital status as a woman" in society "should" be (which my friend Shelley Brown calls total "BullShould"). Maybe you're struggling to be respected for your "unconventional" or even your "conventional" lifestyle choices. Whatever it is, the next time you find yourself smack-dab inside a scenario that calls for conflict before resolution, can you remember to prepare yourself for the frustrating truth that there is likely no "perfect" outcome where everyone gets what he or she wants and lives Disney ever after?

And yet the loveliest reality about sticking by your audacious choices, about walking in your BDE, is that if the people you're engaging with—whether it's parents, roommates, bosses, clients, neighbors, partners, or friends—if they love you, if they are truly your people, they *will* come around. It might take a while. In the case of my parents, if they're being honest, they still don't *love* my decision, but they respectfully accept it. It still feels really awful to know deep down that I've let them down, but what was my other option? To give in and fold on what I wanted for my own life? To be miserable and make everyone else around me mega-miserable? Nope. And therein lies the paradox.

The uncomfortable certainty of a Big Deal life is that once you start (or just keep) swimming in the opposite direction from the rest of your school, you can pretty much count on finding yourself in neither a win-win nor a lose-lose. You're in the uncomfortable purgatory of somewhere in between. And that is the paradox of living an audacious life. You're stoked that you stood by your choice and are living the life that you've designed and that you deserve. But you're simultaneously sad that you've let down or disappointed anyone you love or respect. And for the record, that sadness is a good thing—it's the empathetic difference between audacious and a-hole. And when you're holding space for both of these diametric opposite emotions simultaneously, the tension from this constant tug-of-war paradox can be utterly exhausting. As Olympic weightlifter Jerzy Gregorek says: "Hard choices, easy life. Easy choices, hard life." Talk about putting up a heavy truth.

Now if you're anything like my dearest friends and family, you might be so generous as to wonder if I'm *sure* I made the right choice. Or maybe you just want to know so that you can know if *you'll* ever feel sure that *you* made the right choice. The raw and vulnerable answer is *of course not*! How could I possibly know if I'll change my mind about something in 20 years when some days it feels like I change my mind every 20 minutes?

Hear me on this—whether you're struggling with having kids or not having kids, adopting children, getting married, getting a fur baby, taking the job, quitting the job, moving, staying put, whatever Big Deal choice you're struggling with, you will likely *never* be 100 percent without a shadow-of-doubt ironclad certain that you won't change your mind. The truth is you might regret the decision that you're currently contemplating or are currently thrilled about. And because intuition is individual, and not collective, only you know what the "right" choice ultimately is for you, right now, in your life, at this moment. While obviously I don't know what the "best" decision for you is, I do know one thing: your chances of happiness skyrocket every time you make a decision to move toward something you know you truly want, versus doing something out of fear that you someday might regret it if you don't.

Your chances of happiness skyrocket every time you make a decision to move toward something you know you truly want, versus doing something out of fear that you someday might regret it if you don't.

#BIGDEALBOOK

When you begin to live a more audacious life, the only certainty is the spectrum of emotional uncertainty that will become your new normal. You'll feel exhilarated with energy and frozen by fear and everything in between. And there's a high probability that one emotion will likely transcend the rest: you, my Big Damn Deal reader, will finally feel *free*. You'll feel breathless, liberated, and rewarded—and a sense of deep delight that only an intentionally aligned life can deliver. You'll also find barriers, traps, trolls, tough calls, dark nights, and probably some loneliness when you step into who you truly are. And those "negatives" are typically par for the course as you set out on your brave new misison, and when you stand up for what *you* want in life. Sometimes you are loaded up with Team Abundance players, but other times you're not. Sometimes it can be incredibly isolating to go left when everyone else is going right.

And here we arrive at the nonsexy fine print that leaves the majority of women more stuck than my jeans zipper after the first few months of the COVID-19 Poundemic. The embarrassing truth about truly audacious life decisions is that sometimes you might feel so desolate being the only one not following the "standard life plan" of your crew that you might be tempted to change your mind just so you'll have some friends left! The need to belong is baked into our DNA. But is that a robust enough reason to betray yourself? To try and silence what it is your soul seeks? In some cases, what it screams? So you'll keep your old friends? So you'll make your parents, your boss, or your team happy at the exchange rate of personal misery? So you won't be the only one "left out"? The price of belonging is steep, and only you can decide if it's worth paying. You might be thinking, *Uh, yeah! Yep! Sure is!* And if so, go for it. That's the beauty of being a woman in a free country in the twenty-first century—you, unlike millions of women in other countries in the world today, possess the privilege of deciding your own destiny.

But before you commit to a life of muting your internal GPS lady in exchange for a packed social calendar and endless Instalikes, remember that if you've ever felt lonely in a crowded room, felt alone even when you were in a relationship, or experienced the excruciating emotions that accompany being the black sheep of your family, you know that just because people physically around you are *with* you and pleased with you does *not* mean that *you* will feel pleased with you.

So which is worse? Only you can answer that question. (See, it really *is* a paradox.)

In the unquestionably best movie of all time, *Bridesmaids*, annoyingly "perfect" Helen is shown reassuring the anxious bride Lillian not to feel bad that they're flying first class while their other friend Annie flies in coach. Helen comforts Lillian by saying, "There's much more of a sense of community in coach, I promise." And while I hate to admit to Helen being right about *anything* after what she pulled with the French-themed shower, she did drop a tough truth bomb about the comfort and connectivity that comes from sitting in the same cozy section as pretty much everyone else. As counterintuitive as it sounds, it can be challenging to fly first class.

When you're audacious enough to make an independent choice, when you decide to shift how you're traveling through life, you may initially feel a loss of community. Sometimes when you've listened to your heart, created a new option, stood by your beliefs, challenged what felt unfair, or gone the road less traveled, you're going to wish you could exchange your ticket midflight. Sometimes you're going to feel guilty that you're drinking free champagne while Annie in coach is glaring at you over her luke-warm $8 Bud Light. Sometimes you'll hear the big laugh from two strangers hitting it off in 23 B and C and wish the important-looking executive next to you wasn't so immersed in that spread-sheet. And in those moments, the only way you will stay the course you've charted for the destination you desire is to get *way* better at being your own bestie. Sometimes you have to play

Helen *and* Lillian *and* Annie—all at once. And that takes cultivating some first-class courage and some serious self-reliance. It takes reminding yourself, especially when you feel yourself wimping out or wavering, that you are kind of a Big Deal. And Big Deal gals don't back down at the first sign of a little turbulence. Especially not in business class.

BE YOUR OWN BESTIE

If you're already an introvert who *loves* being alone, you know better than most that there is a difference between being *alone* and being *lonely*. Maybe your idea of a perfect Friday night is to curl up with a good book, order takeout, and ignore the world. Good for you! If you're an extrovert though, you may have just found yourself experiencing a little bit of what can only be described as a heart palpitation. So for you, my extrovert reader, let's unpack precisely how you can become better at being alone, become better at being your own bestie.

As a side note: If you're currently finding yourself experiencing feelings of deep sadness, depression, or anxiety, or where you're already spending more time alone than is healthy, this chapter is not the right help for you. I'm an entrepreneur who writes books about my experiences and what I know to be true for me and those I've encountered, but I'm certainly nowhere near the remote realm of any kind of doctor. Please, *please* reach out to a professional to help you cope with those emotions. And if you find you can't afford therapy right now, there are dozens and dozens of telemental health apps monitored by professionals 24/7 for immediate assistance at a much lower cost than traditional therapy. You can visit https://www.psycom.net/25-best-mental-health-apps to get started. You are not alone. People care about you. ***Please promise you'll seek the professional help required for your situation.***

Let's say maybe you're someone who has never eaten out alone at a restaurant? Or that one time you did, you vowed never again? Or maybe you're someone who despises yoga and meditation because you would rather go to the DMV on Friday at noon than be alone with only your thoughts for even five minutes?

I get it, because coming from a big, loud Irish family that I adore, I used to be a classic extrovert. Coming from a family of storytellers, creatives, musicians, and the most beautiful *big* personalities, I was conditioned to understand that whoever talks the loudest gets heard the most. (It wasn't until later in life that I realized my default "speaking" decibel was actually categorized by most as "shouting.") Maybe you grew up in a family where every birthday, milestone, sacrament, and even the small wins all warranted a massive gathering with everyone involved in everyone else's business—all the time. Interrupting is just how we converse. Teasing is how we express love. Exaggeration is an art form. Toasting to the ups and the downs is just culturally how we live. Picture *My Big Fat Greek Wedding* but swap plates of gyros for pints of Guinness.

So it's no big surprise that coming from that type of clan, I went through most of my adult life with a massive circle of acquaintances and a packed social calendar. And, *yes*, there are endless benefits to surrounding yourself with community and relationships that lift you up. There's nothing more important than having a laugh with the ones you love and showing up when people need you the most. This is why most of us—yes, even the introverts at some point—went semi-mad in full quarantine, because we're all inherently social creatures who long to hug, touch, and connect. (In varying amounts, of course.) Even in the Blue Zones of the world—those mysterious locations with incredible concentrations of centenarians—their longevity is attributed to genetics and diet, but most importantly, the scientists who study them have found that one of the commonalities of those who live past 100 is a deep sense of connectedness and *community*.

And maybe for you, managing to maintain an extremely huge network at a high level without missing a beat or a birthday is a piece of cake. That is 100 percent my sister-in-law Lauren, and if she didn't always write and send the most thoughtful, warm, and emotional cards, I would swear she was a multitasking robot programmed for organizational perfection. (And, yes, I'm jealous, and I'm convinced she has a backup army of elves somewhere just planning, and wrapping, and mailing.) My sister Shannon is the same way, effortlessly making every person in her vast social circle feel seen, and heard, and special. (If this is also you, it's truly an impressive talent.)

While your level of socialization is obviously totally unique to your life and your preferences, like many of us who have decided to use our audacity to end a relationship (romantic or otherwise), quit an old habit, remove an unhealthy obstacle, move to a new place, start a new venture, or even just set new boundaries, you may find yourself initially struggling with the emotional component of being more alone than you're used to (or comfortable with) as you engineer a new existence, a new environment, or a new way of truly embracing your unique brand of Big Deal Energy.

And this evolution typically happens not clearly and quickly, but much more stealthily. I'll never forget when my professional speaking career started to take off, over the course of a few months it seemed like I went from someone with a "usual" order at my local coffee shop where I would meet friends regularly, to this person who was ordering something new, every day, in whichever city I was in, in a packed coffee shop full of strangers. (Anyone else flummoxed by a flat white?) I went from someone who traveled with family or friends for vacay nearly quarterly, to a full-time solo business traveler. Slowly, I found I couldn't meet friends for brunch, make someone's birthday dinner, or join the workout crew, because I was always out of town. So naturally, the invitations slowed . . . and then eventually stopped.

Now, don't get me wrong; I'm not playing the world's tiniest violin here, as I *love* to travel and pinch myself on the regular that my dream job is exactly what I'm already doing. *And yet*, within the first two years of saying yes to building this new full-time global speaking business, I found my friend group shrank dramatically to the smallest it had ever been in my entire life. And when I was home, instead of rushing to see my friends as I thought I would, I found myself needing to physically recharge from the trip. I needed sleep, veggies, and husband time. And just when I felt like full-capacity me again, it was time to leave for the next gig in the next city.

So whether you are jet-setting, carving out time for a new hobby, or embarking upon some overdue self-discovery, making the space to do this work will likely feel lonely and even a little eerie at first. And when you find yourself wrestling with Big Deal desolation, you'll discover solace in the practice of being better at being your own bestie. How? Here are a few ideas . . .

Reframe How You Think About Yourself

The first way to begin to get better at being your own bestie (whether for a temporary period of time or not) is to reframe how you think about being alone. Being alone isn't inherently a good or evil state; instead, it takes on the categorization that you choose to give it. If you find yourself thinking, *Ugh, I'm so lonely,* one quick flip of the script would be to correct yourself and say something along the lines of, *You know, I'm really enjoying this restorative time of solitude.* Then try to practice a moment of radical gratitude for something right there in front of you that is only available to you because you're alone. That you're wearing your ugliest, comfiest sweatpants with the utmost confidence. Or that you're reading a trashy romance novel in peace without worrying about people judging the cover. Or that you can actually go for a walk without stressing about what time you have to get back. Or that you can just take a minute and be "off duty" without having to search for conversation topics to fill any silences.

If that's hard for you to do, can you try to remember that you aren't a weirdo whom no one likes; you're simply not making other people the absolute highest priority at this particular moment. And that's OK. (And, *no*, nothing is wrong with you!)

Learn What's Really Important to *You*

The second way to get better at being your own bestie is to get to know yourself better. Without having to put everyone else's needs and opinions there right alongside yours, you might discover a few things you didn't even know you preferred, valued, or straight-up *needed*.

For example, my husband is not a big sleeper, nor are some of my family members, or really any of my friends, to be honest. I remember growing up and people bragging about being up at 5 a.m. as if it were a badge of honor. Most of my core people run just fine on five to six hours, kids or no kids. Many of them are night owls as well who like to meet for 8 p.m. dinners, New York style. Even my 82-year-old father-in-law refuses to have dinner before 8 p.m. for fear of being an "old person"! So I just always thought that was how I like to operate as well. But one night I was staying in a hotel by myself for a gig in New Orleans, and I woke up in the exact same position after sleeping through the night for nine hours straight! I remember bounding out of bed and feeling so flustered, confused, and . . . ashamed. I legit checked my phone in a panic, hoping no one called and would have found out that I was lazy Lady of Leisure–ing it up. What kind of wimpy, weak, slacker-to-the-max adult sleeps nine hours and loves it? But I saw the difference in everything almost instantly that day. My skin, my energy, my attitude, my productivity. It was literally one of the best days of my life!

So I've come to embrace the fact that, professional non-sleeping overachievers be damned, I am just one of those humans where the amount of sleep I get really, really matters when it comes to overall life quality. The more sleep I get, the more I feel clear, focused, and energized. And yet, talking about loving getting those eight hours of sleep consistently doesn't win you any awards in the respect or likability department, unfortunately. It's almost shameful in our "hustle until you no longer have to introduce yourself" culture!

Maybe for you, you don't really like eating a ton of sweets, but you live or work in a place where it's always around and everyone else hazes you into partaking.

Maybe you've spent your life eating meat, gossiping, working out, shopping, doing home projects, organizing, or whatever else and realize once you're alone that maybe wasn't really actually your jam after all? Is there something in your life that you've been subscribing to that on second glance might be time to unsubscribe to? Or maybe you've been harboring a secret urge to create sexy roller-skating TikTok videos set to Stevie Nicks's greatest hits but were paralyzed by the inevitability of people judging you for being too [insert negative adjective here] to do so? What if you went all in on the doing and the seeing and the learning with what you truly enjoy? I dare you to pay attention to what came to mind for you just now, and I dare you to freaking go your own way and *do it*! (Then please DM me on Instagram as soon as you do.)

Set Goals That Actually Matter to *You*

The third way to get better at being your own bestie is to set internal, accolade-focused goals. How can you do a better job making yourself proud? Most of us have been ensnared at one time or another in the expectations of everyone—from our parents to our partners—that we forget to even define what it is we expect from ourselves. What does success really truly look like *to you*? Is it the same vision that you were taught was the path when you were a child? Is it the "standard-issue life plan" route? Is it placing the same value on what your friends do in terms of material items or certain milestones? Are you doing the next extreme Instagram fitness challenge because you really want to or because everyone else is hazing you into it? Is it something vague like "I just want to feel happy," or is it something measurable like "I'm going to put on my old Irish dancing shoes and hop around like a little loony leprechaun in my garage for at least one hour a week because even though I'm old and I suck at it and everyone would think it's totally weird, I don't care, because it brings me joy"? (What? That's not your go-to hobby?)

Maybe your answer that came to mind had to do with making six, seven, eight, or twenty figures a year. And if that was your answer, yay! Do it. Fair warning: I always thought success meant having a certain amount of money and a certain lifestyle. And that people who said, "Well, money isn't everything," or "Money can't buy happiness," were just jealous broke people who didn't know any better. So rude, right? Well, one year I earned the most money I'd ever earned in my life (to this day!) and I swear to you, I have never been more miserable. I had night terrors; my hair was falling out in the shower; I stopped getting my period. I was chained to my investors, my clients, and my employees, and I was *drowning* in obligation. I even visited my parents once during this time and instead of spending quality time with them, golfing, visiting, being present, and unplugging, I couldn't. Why? Because all that money turned out to come with a thick, unbreakable pair of golden handcuffs. Stuck in back-to-back-to-back calls, not enjoying any of the special time. I remember running to the kitchen to grab a quick glass of water and seeing my parents' dog just sleeping lazily on the porch in the middle of a Monday morning and feeling jealous of the freaking *dog*. I hope you're hearing me when I say chewing bones on the floor sounded like *heaven* compared to the 12 back-to-back meetings of problems and drama I had facing me that day.

It wasn't until after one very scary full-on mental breakdown panic attack in the shower that scared not only me, but Hartman as well, that I knew something drastic had to be done. I blew up the business model, laid off two-thirds of my staff, lost a ton of revenue, and decided to entirely reinvent my lifestyle and my business. I was judged, sued, and hated. Family and friends would come visit me in my new digs, and the sympathy on their faces was obvious (*Is she seriously living in this little crappy apartment? At her age? She had been doing so well.*)

But what they didn't know was that I was finally, *actually*, doing better than well. Because I gained something that I now realize is how I truly define success: *freedom.* To the world, it looked like a downgrade. But I knew that all I felt was an upgrade. What made me proud of myself was creating a life by design that gives me the freedom to do the things I love: reading, writing, creating, mountain biking, surfing, playing my guitar, and most importantly, having the space to spend quality time with the people I love most are priceless compared to making five times the money and having five times nicer things. And I've still never come close to making that amount of money again. But I've also never come close to being that miserable ever again, either.

When you examine your goals and objectives for this week, this month, this year, or five years from now, what does success truly look like *for you*? If your parents or your friends or your neighbors or whoever else influences your definition of success didn't get a say, if they couldn't weigh in and approve or not, would your goals still look the same? If you accomplished everything on your list right now, and then someone told you that today was your last day on earth, how would you feel about what you prioritized spending your time on? Regretful? Frantic? Freaked out? As your own bestie, maybe it's time to get crystal clear on what you are chasing down and, even more important, why? Maybe it's time to revisit some of these goals, just for a little quality control, and perhaps have the audacity to cross out, rewrite, or add specifics to them (which we'll tackle shortly in this chapter's Big Deal Diary).

KEEP ON KEEPIN' ON

So you might be wondering, what if you set out with awesomely audacious goals and you made bold choices, but now that you're deep in the nonsexy loneliness of execution, you're having audacity remorse? What should you do, not if but *when* your resolve starts to fade? This is where things get a little tricky.

No offense to Dori from *Finding Nemo*, but "Just keep swimming" seems easier to do if you have a strange amnesia allowing you to selectively forget negative experiences and tough challenges. *What debt? What lawsuit? What boss from hell? What coworker from Smugtown? What annoying neighbor?*

What judgy parent? Oops! I forgot! Of course, we all want to be grittier and more resilient; we all want to be able to persevere through anything—why do you think we live for Insta power quotes? #ProgressNotPerfection.

But the reality is that while starting something new is exciting, and diving into the unknown is exhilarating, when things start to crash and burn and life gets *real*, that high can turn into the lowest and the loneliest of the low feelings in an instant. You might even feel so low that you convince yourself of the falsehood that everyone else had the right idea all along after all. *So this is why my parents are disappointed. This is why my friends think I've lost my mind. This is why my siblings, or neighbors, or coworkers have been "judgy concerned"* (the worst of the *"whys"*).

As I mentioned earlier in the story with my parents, it's so tempting—like "a pizza when you're on a healthy eating program" level of tempting—to just give in and give up. Especially when you know that you are bringing this on yourself. It's kind of madness to know that if you really wanted to, you could easily opt back out at any point! And when you're back at that intersection between Where You Were Street and Where You're Heading Way, revisit your original goal. Your end game. Your impact. Your success vision. And if you still feel that tug on your heart, if that inner GPS lady is still repeating over and over again "Turn left" no matter which buttons you push to shut her up, then unfortunately, my friend, you just can't. (Well, you *can*, but you'll probably go insane from all the nagging she will do for the rest of your life.)

When you start to freak out about the realities of reinvention that accompany your big audacious decision, take a deep breath and remember just how much you trust yourself. You didn't make these waves, these choices, and these changes to have a lonely, sad existence. You made them because you're ready to experience firsthand what's on the other side of fear. Using your Big Deal Energy, you know that you *will* keep swimming—with or without the convenient Dory amnesia to lighten the load for you.

When you start to freak out about the realities of reinvention that accompany your big audacious decision, take a deep breath and remember just how much you trust yourself.

#BIGDEALBOOK

WHEN YOU'VE CHANGED YOUR MIND

But what if you change your mind? What if you find yourself down this bumpier, potholed road less traveled and discover that you actually liked the other smooth, newly paved road better all along? Maybe you've realized that the "standard life plan" is actually looking pretty fantastic right about now. Well, it's simple: Changing your mind is not just allowed; it's encouraged. If you've become privy to new data or circumstances, staying the course on a sinking ship is not called resilience; it's called a really bad idea. (FYI: men change their minds all the time; they are just better at doing it unapologetically by disguising it with horrendous corporate buzzwords like *pivot*.) So while there's nothing inherently wrong with changing your mind, there is something unwise about not putting in the work to discern the why behind the U-turn. Are you changing your mind because the outcome isn't delivering what you expected? Or are you changing your mind because you're scared and lonely? If it's the first, better to fail fast and reinvent faster. But if it's the latter . . . I recommend outlining two scenarios.

For the first scenario, I want you to think about what initially got you going down this path. Why was the internal GPS lady so insistent on you traveling this way in the first place? Now think about what your life would look like if you followed this direction all the way until you reach your final destination (for this trip, anyway!). How does that place feel for you?

For the second scenario, imagine that you just give up. You're not admitting defeat or failure; you've quite simply just decided to *veer* or *swivel*. Now, imagine what your life will look like if you "pivot" back to the way things were? Start remembering all the things that may have changed, and the people who may have been inspired or influenced along the way. How do you feel when you visualize what that life would look like now?

One of the greatest ways to gain clarity when you find yourself stuck at this crossroads is to perform a facts-versus-feelings exercise. We'll be deep-diving into this in our Big Deal Diary prompts later, but let's get warmed up now with this clarifying query: Are you truly separating the objective facts from your subjective feelings? Facts like *Well it's too expensive* or *It's taking too long* aren't nearly as important as tuning into your feelings like *I feel content but not thrilled* or *I feel a little nervous but mostly exhilarated and alive*. On the flip side, what if you find yourself drowning in your feelings like *I just feel so over-whelmed*, but the reality is that you've actually managed to decrease how much time you spend doing tasks you abhor, or that you've started to better manage your time, or that you've accomplished your sales or friendship goals? That fact can counter and reframe this feeling because maybe the truth is that you actually *aren't* that overwhelmed after all.

The paradox likely continues in that neither of the directions is probably a clear-cut, simple emotion or foolproof set of feelings. But the beauty of being your own bestie is that you know how to authorize yourself to trust that *you do know what to do.* But, of course, it's up to you: Do you still want to change your mind, or will you audaciously continue to press forward and chase down the future you that will likely stay pleasantly persistent until you heed her call? As always, it's up to you.

THE PARADOX OF THE PARADOX

So far, we've been looking at this from only our point of view . . . but what about when you're on the other side of it all? When maybe you're the one who has stopped calling that friend because she's always too busy chasing down her dream to make time for you? Or maybe when you're the one left behind while she goes in search of the life she wants for herself? Just as there are two sides to every coin, there are two sides to audacious living. Being audacious enough to chase something down in spite of how the world responds is one side. The other side? That's having the audacity to accept and support someone else's mission—especially when it's the polar opposite of your own.

I'll never forget when one of my best friends, Madeline, decided she wanted to completely change her life, and I mean *completely*. Follow me down this story: For years, she spent her weekdays crushing her high-six-figure corporate healthcare job. She rocked it *and* somehow managed to make it to the 10 a.m. Barry's Bootcamp session on weekdays between meetings. On the weekends, she was a Cali Coachella gal, wearing onesies and roller-skating around to epic beach parties. Picture Kate Hudson circa *Almost Famous* but more adventuresome and more financially savvy. She climbed Mount Kilimanjaro. She would jet to Mexico City for the weekend to brave a new speakeasy. She skied Vail and Aspen and Jackson Hole. We traveled all around Italy together, drinking the most beautiful wine and meeting the most fascinating people.

Then one day, she decided she wanted a new life. No major event trigger. No major epiphany moment. She just knew she *wanted* to. Her audacious inner GPS lady was calling an audible, and Madeline heeded the call. Just like that, over the span of two years, with shocking speed, she quit her job, moved across the country back to the South, bought a huge house, became a stay-at-home mom of two, and is *loving* her new life attending Junior League meetings and country club galas. Madeline went on an audacious mission and straight-up traded in a set of skates for a set of pearls.

And this is where things get awkward. I'm ashamed to admit that instead of my knee-jerk reaction being "*Yay!* Go, Madeline! Team Abundance all day!," I was confused. Sad. Bummed.

Maybe even a little . . . I'm ashamed to say this . . . judgy? Was she going backward? How could she give up her impressive career? Wouldn't she be bored? What about her love of travel? Will she still be a shocking storyteller? How would *my* life without my most legendary friend be impacted? Because, remember, big changes ignite big reactions. I'll never forget boo-hooing about all these (extremely selfish) questions to my dad one night. He looked at me like I was a total jerk and said, "E, seriously? Get over it! It's her life, not yours. Come on. You're better than that." Ouch.

But, as usual, Dad was right. In my mind, she wasn't living the life that *I* wanted her to live, the life that in *my* opinion was the more exciting and braver, the life that I thought was more fulfilling of her incredible potential. Kinda like my parents felt about my child-free choice. And the truth is that while our occasional FaceTimes don't even come close to the epic friendship we used to have, and I miss her being in my life on an everyday basis, she is hands-down the happiest I've ever seen her. She is living the life she was born to live.

And there's the paradox of the paradox: you can be selfishly heartbroken that your bestie has left you, changed, moved on, started something, or quit something and simultaneously be *thrilled* that she's living a life she legitimately loves. And so if you're experiencing something similar right now with one of your dear friends, just remember that Team Abundance players dance joyfully for their friends' big adventures. Even if it is country music. Or that new country-rap hybrid music. And ya'll better believe I'm here for it. And I hope you are too.

⇉ BIG DEAL DIARY ⇇

As you read through the following questions, listen to yourself for the first answers that come to mind for you. Write your answers freely, without judgin, for at least three pages:

✳ How good are you at being alone without being lonely, would you say? (Scale from 1 to 10, where 1 is you *hate* to be alone and 10 is you love a solo movie night . . . or month.)

✳ When you think about living more audaciously, do you have enough time and space in your life to really do so? If yes, yay! If not, how might you create more time and space for yourself today or this week?

✳ How well do you know yourself?

  ↺ What do you think you need more of in your life?

  ↺ What do you need less of?

  ↺ What do you value most?

  ↺ Facts versus feelings—how well can you separate the reality of a situation, person, or thing from the way you feel about a situation, person, or thing?

✳ How well do you know what you expect from yourself?

  ↺ What does success look like for you?

- How closely do you feel you are currently achieving those expectations?

- Are you proud of yourself?

- If *sort of* or *no*, what could you do to get that answer closer to yes?

✷ How well are you supporting or at least accepting the Team Abundance players in your life who are polar opposite to you in terms of life preferences and priorities?

#BIGDEALBOOK

CHAPTER 9

YOUR PARTY, YOUR PLAYLIST

I magine for a second that you are hosting a summer dinner party at your house. Your charcuterie plate is Pinterest-worthy. Your outfit is fabulous. Your Spotify playlist—Jack Johnson Beach Jams—is the perfect background soundtrack to set the mood for open, relaxed conversation. And in this mellow moment—you are the world's most superb hostess. Until suddenly, one of the guests inexplicably grabs your phone, changes the playlist to Dave's Dive Bar Favs, and cranks it up. Oh, *no he didn't*. Everyone knows that (1) it is *way* too early for Journey and (2) when it's your party, it's *your playlist*.

And it's my hope *that* is the final message you take away from the pages of this book and into your Big Deal life starting right now. If there is someone in your life who keeps changing the metaphorical soundtrack of your life—without your OK—will you choose to unleash your newly unlocked (or refreshed) audaciousness and put a stop to that vibe hijacking *stat*? It's not OK at a soiree, and it's *really* not OK in the story of your life.

In those crucial life montage moments, when maybe you find yourself being shamed, mocked, jinxed, or rooted against simply because you didn't take life at its face value, you will be tempted to hand over your Spotify password so others can control the music and volume of your life (it's easier that way, after all).

Please, please, *please* reject all attempts from external hostile forces to commandeer that kind of control over your life. Protect that password and play your favs—whether it's Italian opera or rap. Whether it's power over your playlist or your life, will you authorize yourself to decide which volume makes the most sense for your current scene?

Let's look at some of the classic life situations where it's likely your resolve will be tested. Being super aware of these potential pitfalls up front is crucial if you want to stop playing small and start playing bigger.

- **Taking a break from the hustle:** Whether you're an entrepreneur or corporate executive, it's such a slippery slope to get sucked into the "sleep when you're dead" hustle culture mentality. If you find yourself in that circle, it takes audacity to admit that you actually like living in the moment, you prioritize sleep, and you value work-life balance over any dollar amount. The horror! If you work hard at your side hustle, like a network marketing organization or freelance work, it takes audacity to defend what you do when interacting with nine-to-five corporate traditionalists looking down on your "gigs" from their fat, company-matched 401(k) retirement stack. It takes those nine-to-five corporate executives' audacity to admit that they actually *love* what they do when they encounter entrepreneurial "Why would you ever work for someone else?" types.

- **Speaking politically:** Depending on where you live in the country or the circles you run in, you'll likely find yourself in a social setting where you are outnumbered by a bunch of extreme liberals in LA or a bunch of mega-conservatives in Texas. No matter which side of the coin you lean toward, it takes huge audacity in those moments where everyone is looking at you like you're crazy to either stand up verbally for what you truly believe in or opt out of the conversation. It takes major BDE to retain the right to express your opinions, whatever those might be. Especially in the era of social media.

- **Parenting:** If you're a parent, it takes audacity to say that you want to also have a career or that you love being a stay at home parent. It also takes audacity to say that you regret having a career or that you regret being a stay at home parent. It takes audacity to say you don't want to do any of it, and it takes audacity to say you want to do all of it.

- **Defining your religion:** If you grew up in a religious family, it takes audacity to leave that religion behind; or if you grew up without spirituality and found God, it takes audacity to ask to say a prayer at family dinner. It takes audacity to stick by your atheism or your personal definition of spirituality.

- **Owning your identity:** Whatever your race, sexual orientation, or preferred pronoun, it takes audacity to own who you are proudly when you are in environments where simply being yourself makes other people "uncomfortable."

- **Being a woman in a male-dominated industry (or vice versa):** If you are in a traditionally male-dominated work environment, it takes audacity to demand equality, to require that you be both liked *and* respected, instead of the usual one or the other.

- **Creating your home:** If you live in your hometown or general region where you grew up, it takes audacity to admit you love the familiarity of where you live to people who have traveled the world and "seen it all."

- **Traveling the world:** It takes audacity for world travelers to face their "settled-down, mortgaged adult" relatives at the holidays who view them as rootless.

- **Age expectations:** It takes audacity to not "act your age" appropriately, whether that's acting much younger or older than you are.

- **Dating:** It takes audacity to date someone your family members don't like or to leave someone they do.

- **Being you:** It takes audacity to truly be who you are because—especially in the age of the internet and social media—someone, somewhere, will always view your choices through their lens and have a dissenting opinion about it.

No matter which songs you select for your Big Deal playlist, add them with certainty. Blare them with pride. Share them with love. Dance like no one is watching or like everyone is watching on TikTok.

REAL TREADMILL TALK

Have you ever run a 5K? How about a half-marathon? If you just wrinkled up your nose, maybe you're someone who has unfollowed friends who post endlessly about their workouts and sweat sessions. I am someone who derives major inspiration from following these fitness freaks, like my brother Brian who recently trained for the Boston marathon. He diligently trained for more than a year. He raised thousands of dollars for cancer research and was *ready* to crush this legendary race. My whole fam booked our flights to cheer him on along the route, and we got the shirts made. It was all very exciting. But when COVID hit, the marathon was canceled for the first time since 1897.

So did Brian decide to eat white Poundemic carbs and rewatch *Stranger Things* on Netflix like the rest of us? Nope. No he did not. Instead, he decided to run the marathon anyway. *Around his neighborhood.* With no competitors or spectators. And most audaciously (insanely?) of all? *With no headphones or music.*

Most people run a marathon in four or five hours. Brian? Three-and-a-half hours. And at the finish line, where people are usually cheering and there are photos and just all-around emotional *epicness*? He just ran back to his driveway. And then he stopped, like when Forrest Gump reaches the end of the Santa Monica Pier.

My brother didn't turn around and run back across the country to Maine, inspiring smiley face t-shirt memes like a modern-day Forrest. Instead, once the fanfare died down, and he blew everyone's minds on social media, and his legs recovered, and marathon training was over, take a wild guess what he decided next? Yep! That he's going to run it again. But this time, 15 minutes faster.

OK, let's pause. Before you roll your eyes because you have *zero* desire in you to replicate this level of discipline, I want to make it clear that I don't either. And yet, it's likely that at some point, you've actually found yourself in a situation not unlike Brian's. Whether you ran a 5K or simply started walking every day, you accomplished a physical goal. Or maybe you got that certification. Or you launched a business. Or you finished a project. Maybe you achieved an emotional goal, like finally, *really* loving the newly single or not-so-newly single life. Maybe you've finally started to relish your reclaimed independence and freedom. Maybe you've been feeling that lately your marriage, partnership, and/or dating life is healthier, more fulfilling, and (hopefully!) more fun. Perhaps your child (or fur baby) is healthy, happy, and/or succeeding. Your parents, parental figures, or mentors are proud. Your boss, board, or investors are thrilled. Your employee is delivering. Your bestie is pleased with her latest news. You finally managed to buy *that thing*. Or even better, let that thing *go*.

Whatever flavor your achievement was, after the initial endorphin rush of summitting that mountaintop, what happened? Just like Brian, maybe you looked around, inhaled the beauty, and then after a few minutes (seconds?) of reveling in your accomplishment, you might have found yourself starting to shift uncomfortably. Maybe you thought to yourself, *Hmm, so now what? What's that over there? An even higher peak? Huh* . . .

Ah, the puzzle of achievement. Or as it's technically called, the *hedonic treadmill* or *hedonic adaptation*. You may have heard of this, but if not, it's essentially our universal human tendency to quickly return to our baseline level of happiness after a major positive (or negative) life change or accomplishment. If you're a goal getter, contemplating this conundrum likely makes you a little uncomfortable. It is a little troubling to process that once we accomplish our goals, our busy minds cannot help but automatically reset the pin a little bit farther, the bar a tad higher, the next milestone a teeny bit bigger. So we continue to rinse and repeat this vicious cycle . . . over and over . . . until . . . I guess, we're dead? Yikes. How depressing is that? Or is it?

No, of course it's not, because what would you propose to do with your precious short time on this earth instead? Couch-blob it up your whole life, rewatching old *Gossip Girl* episodes, and ordering Postmates Thai noodles, because who cares—you're just going to die anyway? That might be fun for a little while, but you probably wouldn't truly feel that you are living a life you love as you scream at Dorota Kishlovsky to grow a backbone and quit working for the Waldorfs for the hundredth time.

Like most things in life, real happiness (for most of us) comes from striking a balance that works for your individual baseline happiness set point. And only *you*—not your family, or your partner, or your friends, or social media—can determine where that set point exists.

Like most things in life, real happiness (for most of us) comes from striking a balance that works for your individual baseline happiness set point. And only you—not your family, or your partner, or your friends, or social media—can determine where that set point exists.

#BIGDEALBOOK

And because intuition is individual, it might be the case that even when you are genetically related to someone, even when you share DNA, it's more often than not that no two of our set points are even remotely alike. For example: My brother's "happy" set point would be a "stressed-out" set point for me. I'll FaceTime him, and there he is, full-time corporate job, a mortgage, three healthy children, and a sweet dog crawling all over him at all times, while he's attempting valiantly to work from home—and instead of looking like someone who is barely keeping it together and praying for cocktail hour, his eyes are crinkled up at the corner with joy, his face clearly telegraphing *how great is this?* He loves the chaos and commotion and mayhem! Thrives at the helm of it! Add that to the fact that the guy also manages to keep in touch with a huge circle of friends from college *and* call our mom most days. He and my sister-in-law, Lauren, absolutely *love* the madness of their adorable little household. Hard work, constant goals, tight deadlines, and extreme achievement make them really *happy*. It works—for them.

On the other hand, my "happy" set point is making a living on creative outputs. For this, I need significant amounts of unstructured time and space for ideas and projects to percolate. That involves a lot more freedom and independence and unknown factors than the average bear, and that's oftentimes judged to high heavens by those who have a very different set point or expectation by which *they* categorize happiness.

Many of my fellow entrepreneurs, business leaders, and authors are master time managers. They are professional time blockers and efficiency hackers. Their eyes bulge out when I share my deep, dark dirty secret that extreme planning makes me feel trapped and sweaty. I prefer to book one-way flights—no more than two weeks in advance. Sometimes I feel overwhelmed with baseline regular adulting like keeping my (fully self-sufficient) grown husband happy and putting everyone's birthday cards in the mail on time(ish). And if you are an über-organizer or a master of your schedule and you're looking down on me from your perfectly color-coordinated highlighted planners and grabbing a snack from your immaculately labeled Tupperware from your walk-in mega-pantry, I honor you. I admire your commitment to your systems. I truly applaud your efficiency, *and* my Big Deal Energy allows me to simultaneously honor my own personal addiction to spontaneity. Maybe you identify more with Brian or more with me or somewhere in between. The good news about this is it truly takes all kinds to make the world go round.

Or maybe you're in a different scenario altogether, because you're someone who *thought* a certain lifestyle would be ideal, but now that you're deep in the thick of it, suddenly you're hearing yourself say negative comments like the awkward, sarcastic "living the dream." Or complaining constantly about how you haven't slept since 2015.

We all have a different set point for how we approach defining goals, living life, and simply existing as a human. How much you crave that sense of pride you feel when you chase down a dream might involve 26.2 miles, 13.1 miles, 3.1 miles, or zero miles. Or maybe you subscribe to the "We're here for a good time, not for a long time" camp. Personally, I'm a huge fan of choice *D*: all of the above. Regardless of how you run or don't run the race, no one knows your ideal soundtrack better than you.

Are you reading this and thinking *marathon*? Are you kidding me? It already feels like I'm running countless laps and just trying to survive my next Zoom call without a child screaming or a dog barking!

If you're dealing with this kind of unhealthy extreme and you're someone who thinks about life as a ladder to be climbed rung by rung, milestone by milestone, until you reach the sky (and, again, you're dead), I offer a different visual to maybe reframe how you think about your journey of life. One that might help you discover a more joyful balance if you haven't already.

What if life isn't to be climbed like a linear ladder straight up? What if it's not to be raced around on a circular track? What if it's more akin to swimming in an unpredictable ocean? One that we tumble around in? We crash on the shore, paddle for waves we miss, and surf the waves we catch. Some days, we're dragged out to sea and held underwater; other days we are relaxing, just floating on the calm surface. Still other days maybe all we can muster is to dip a toe in and scamper back to our towels till it warms up a bit. Depending on where you are on your journey, maybe your version of being audacious is the opposite of all those things. Maybe you're in a season—it could be personal, professional, or collective, like the pandemic—where doing none of the things is what your soul actually needs right now. Maybe you're walking away from our time together with a renewed commitment to subtracting, not adding. Remember that even one strategic "stop" can oftentimes activate even more momentum in your life than a long laundry list of "starts."

Remember that even one strategic "stop" can oftentimes activate even more momentum in your life than a long laundry list of "starts."

#BIGDEALBOOK

Might I suggest you consider borrowing the mentality of a set of humans who log more hours in the ocean than the rest of us (minus boaters)— I'm referring to surfers. These beautiful humans don't even borrow any capes. They're too cool for shirts, let alone capes. But sometimes surfers get caught inside of what's called a "cleanup" set. That's when a series of much larger waves randomly break farther outside than normal, with each wave growing in size and intensity and "cleaning up," or washing away the surfers out of the lineup. While a few lucky ones paddle like hell and just barely make it over the top right before the crash, most of the surfers who didn't see it coming are trapped "inside."

What's that like? Well, you're held under by the force of the waves and swept around in a relentless whitewashing machine. You steal small breaths, trying not to swallow seawater. It's so disorienting that sometimes you'll think you're swimming toward the surface only to discover you're accidentally swimming down deeper while running out of air. When this happens, your natural instinct is to fight like hell, swim as hard as you can, and struggle with all your might to stay afloat.

But smart surfers know that when the ocean is *so* churned up, swimming like hell is actually the fastest way to drown. Wasting your energy and your oxygen trying to fight building-sized monsters of water that are coming down on you is a rookie mistake. So what do the experienced surfers do? They intentionally do the opposite of what their primal brains are screaming at them. They embrace the loss of control. They force their minds to relax. They voluntarily let the waves wash them up, down, and around in countless directions. They wait for their chance to grab a slow, calm breath of as much oxygen as possible, and then they let the ocean do what it will. They embrace the fact that we can't really control anything fully in our lives except our reactions.

These surfers *refuse* to panic. They go on an undesirable, unsolicited, uncontrollable ride because they know the only way to survive is to embrace the terror, accept the uncertainty, and wait for the set to pass. Because cleanup sets don't last forever.

And if you're in a season or a situation that feels like a cleanup set, know that it won't last forever either. Like even the most monstrous cleanup sets, it will pass. Big Deal Energy for you might be requiring your mind to relax when everyone around you is demanding you get worked up. It might mean relinquishing the illusion of control when others are advising that you tighten up the reins. It might mean flowing with the madness when the world tells you not to. Because your inner surfer knows that when you're strategic with your energy, you'll have enough oxygen to not just survive this stormy set, but rise back up to the surface. Your inner surfer knows how to take a deep inhale, catch the next wave, and enjoy the exhilarating ride back to shore.

BUT DID YOU DIE?

Whether you've actually experienced a near-death experience or you've just Googled yourself into being convinced your end is near, you know that at the end of the day, so much of what we've been talking about in this chapter—the achievables, the stressors, the lists, the material goods and goals—doesn't even register in the long run. You don't cry reading a strong P&L report during a eulogy at a funeral. You cry recalling moments of love, kindness, and beauty. You laugh over tales of adventure, cheeky comebacks, and awkward stages.

241

As morbid as it sounds, I *love* thinking about death. In fact, to just lean harder into weirding you out further, I think daily about dying. Daily! And as macabre as that is, apparently I'm not alone, as there's even a term for finding joy in thinking about one's own death. (Whew.) As Ryan Holiday, an author who preaches the ancient concept of Stoicism, writes, "Memento Mori [remember, you too will die] is a reminder to be in the present moment. It's that jolt of happiness when you realize you can let go of trivial matters."

As Holiday further shares this passage from the Roman emperor Marcus Aurelius, "Concentrate on living what can be lived (which means the present) . . . then you can spend the time you have left in tranquility. And in kindness. And at peace with the spirit within you."

That's what we're all really after, isn't it? All the books and the podcasts and the journaling and the action and the challenges are all in search of meaningful existence where the ratio of what really matters versus what does not *feel right*. When you reflect on your inevitable death, it helps to focus your feelings on what you truly prioritize with your time on this planet. My bizarre obsession with daily intentional death contemplation (yep, that's a thing now) didn't arise from casually browsing Stoicism in my down time, but actually started back in 2014 when I was 100 percent convinced I was going to die.

It was 2014, and I was on a dream vacation with Hartman in Europe (who I was so sure was going to propose—he didn't), when I straight-up fainted on the street in Nice, France and was sent to a hospital. (Not from the lack of a ring presentation.) No one spoke English at this hospital; I just remember being in and out of consciousness, hearing people chirping, "Fint? Fint? What is fint?" And me trying to say "Faint!" before promptly "finting" again.

Not knowing what else to do, Hartman and I walked out of the hospital only for me to "fint" again in the ancient cobblestone street right outside the hospital. If you've ever had a true medical emergency with the realization that there is no professional medical help available, and that you are on your own to figure it out, you know the only way to describe the feeling of that experience is sheer terror. After alternately fainting and vomiting on what felt like 19 planes to get home to American soil—and American healthcare—the doctors on this side of the pond were equally puzzled as their French counterparts.

Thus began a nightmare, three-year process of seeing every specialist under the sun in the search for what was wrong with me. MRIs, bloodwork, every test you can imagine—nothing could explain my ongoing symptoms. Finally, I was diagnosed with Meniere's disease, which is caused by a virus that makes you suffer from vertigo and a bunch of weird inner-ear-type stuff.

I'll never forget, *before* my diagnosis, I was in the shower one day after a particularly expensive and fruitless month of testing, and I decided to diagnose myself. The result? I was dying. This party was over. My immediate reaction was *terror*, panic, and a solid full-body boo-hoo. My second reaction? Urgency. Clarity. Calm. What was I going to do with the time I had left?

Almost instantly, a game plan formed. It was a montage of more quality time laughing with friends and family. I saw crazy adventures in Costa Rica, New Zealand, and Greece. I thought about getting Estrogenza going again—this was an annual event when all the women in our family go to the beach, drink wine, and just spend time with each other. Mostly, I thought about all the love I wanted to give my husband, who experienced severe emotional and psychological trauma before the age of 25 from losing both his dad to cancer *and* his first fiancée to mental illness. I started thinking of all these ideas for how to make sure the rest of our time was full of laughs and wild, in-the-moment, spontaneous adventures. And lots and lots of kindness, grace, and love.

My life changed as a result of that false self-diagnosis. It was the most clarifying, motivating, effective strategy to figure out exactly what mattered most in my life—my people. Therein lies the *why* behind our tendency to settle into stuckness despite knowing better and wanting more. This is exactly why even though you know audacity is the answer to breaking through to the other side of the life you were born to live, you come up short. Because it's the people in our lives—our friends, family, neighbors, and even clients—who truly matter when we're staring our mortality in the face. And the fear of losing them, or letting them down, is what paralyzes us from pursuing our wildest dreams.

It's the people in our lives—our friends, family, neighbors, and even clients—who truly matter when we're staring our mortality in the face. And the fear of losing them, or letting them down, is what paralyzes us from pursuing our wildest dreams.

#BIGDEALBOOK

Because we fear losing their respect, or their love, or their approval, we become stuck in a cycle of fear—and we can ride that cycle, but we're neither getting any slimmer from it nor going *anywhere*. Instead, we're spinning our wheels. I hope and pray that it doesn't take a near-death (or even kind of an adjacent death) experience to wake you up and break you out, to help you realize who and what's important. The definition of insanity is doing the same thing over and over and expecting a different result (that and driving on any freeway in California during rush hour).

As you go out into the world, brimming with BDE for days, and you find that your inner GPS lady has malfunctioned or you've listened and listened and you're *still* getting just crickets and dusty tumbleweeds, this last bit of Big Deal Diary work is *exactly* what you need to trigger your intuition into revealing the people, the places, and the choices in which you truly want to be investing your precious "life-or-death" time and energy. And it's my hope you discover some fresh perspectives and unearth some hidden crucial observations that only you are in the position to truly see.

⇒ BIG DEAL DIARY ⇐

This is our last Big Deal Diary, and I'm a little misty about it. And considering the subject matter of our reflections here, you might get a little misty, too. But don't worry. The focus here isn't on death itself. It's on reinvention. It's on coming to some big realizations so that you can use the lessons in this book to channel your best Elle Woods bend and snap and pivot from ice luges to Ivy League.

As you read through the following questions, listen to yourself for the first answers that come to mind for you. Write your answers freely, without judging, for at least three pages:

✳ **You're dying.** Imagine for a moment that you are on your deathbed. What is the *second* emotion you feel? The first will, of course, likely be panic, but what is the second emotion?

   ಅ Where does your mind go?

   ಅ What do you regret?

   ಅ Wish for?

   ಅ Worry about?

   ಅ Feel sad about?

✳ **You're not dying.** Now remind yourself that you are *not* dying at this exact moment (well technically yes, and you never know, but for the most part not right now!)

- ⦿ Where could you spend more time just enjoying moments with people, places, activities?

- ⦿ Can you pick one person, place, or thing to just simply *enjoy* by the end of the day?

✳ **Make failure fun.** When you are in pursuit of something or someone, technically you are in a state of failure until you achieve it. When you think about the person or thing you are chasing right now, can you call to mind one thing you could do to enjoy your "state of failure" more? If you are chasing a weight-loss goal, can you sit down for an extra few minutes after your workout, and instead of checking your phone, just close your eyes, feel the sweat and the endorphins, and thank your body for serving you with strength? Can you smile and enjoy the post-workout pride for right now—instead of waiting for five pounds from now?

✳ **Mantra anchor.** Pick your mental mantra to help you anchor your thoughts toward gratitude, joy, and enjoying the right here, right now. With mantras, just saying them isn't enough. Repeat them until you *feel* the *feeling*. For me, it's a quick shiver of energy. Sometimes your heart flutters or your face smiles without trying. Here are some of my favorites for you to borrow. Simply write them down, repeat them out loud, and wait for the feels:

- "I am here. I am now. I am enough."

- "I am here now. I'll be there later."

- "I will figure it out. For now, I'm at peace."

- "I am so grateful for this moment right now."

- "Exhale the past; inhale the future. I'm so thankful to exist in between those two right now."

- "The only thing that is *real* is *right now*."

- "I have what it takes right now, where I am."

#BIGDEALBOOK

YOUR VOLUME IS UP TO YOU

s you get further into your audacious adventure, you might find yourself asking, *how* audacious is *too* audacious? Can too much audacity venture into a-hole territory? Or what if I'm not audacious enough? How will I know where the line lies?

Now, without giving the classic vague consulting answer ("It depends"), the answer is . . . well, shoot—it depends. Channeling your BDE for maximum positive results comes down to how you respond to barriers, red lights, and roadblocks standing in your way. Maybe you need to turn your audacity down to slowly go around a fallen tree. Maybe you need to turn it up to pass a super-slow car in front of you. Like deciding to turn up the tunes for a road trip sing-along or turning down the music for a soothing dinner party background—your volume is up to you. It's subjective. It's personal. And only you can decide what it is. And it also varies! You'd get a headache listening to even your favorite jams at full blast for hours and hours on end. But more often than not, there's a good chance that you might need to dial up your BDE a notch. You might need to turn up your truth. Turn up your courage. Turn up your resolve. Turn up your creativity. Because the audacious woman in you knows that it is your choice and your choice *only* to take that knob and dial it to a unique volume that empowers you to show up as your most powerful, authentic, divine, Big Deal self.

And if people don't like it?

Well, with all due respect, they can just kiss your audacity.

ACKNOWLEDGMENTS

Publishing a book is like reliving your middle school years. It takes about three years from ideation to publication. You have no idea what you're doing. You feel like everyone is staring at you and whispering about you behind your back for your stupid outfit choice, dumb comment in class, or a hundred other narratives that are not remotely happening in reality. Every day feels like you are about to get your (first) period. It's like riding an actual hormonal roller coaster where, in the span of just one school week, you can go from fully in love to devastated, back to flirting, and back to heartbroken again. Everything is dramatic and extra, and the feels are for reals. You're embarrassed; you're pumped; you're hopeless; you're ecstatic; you're frustrated; you're bored; you're never alone; you're lonely. No one understands you, and yet there are other times you feel completely seen. It's absolute inconsistent chaos, which is exactly how writing this book felt to me. Doesn't it sound *sooooo* fun to hang out with someone reliving a middle school mentality in her late thirties? Yeah, exactly. And for that reason, this Acknowledgments section contains the most important words of this entire book. If you're reading this and you are one of the individuals who had the love, loyalty, and creativity (and quite possibly temporary insanity) to stick by me throughout a process this tumultuous—you deserve to be canonized. Or at least preserved for posterity in print. So before they start playing the walk-off music . . .

First, an enormous thank you to my readers. You didn't just inspire this book; you invented it. Let's just say you all really put the *direct* in *direct messaging* and I deeply honor your audacity in doing so. Yes, we first fell in love back in 2017 with *Digital Persuasion: Sell Smarter in the Modern Marketplace,* but it was your DMs after I gave after speaking at your conventions on digital communications where you really held my feet to the fire. After almost every event, a weird phenomenon kept occuring. You would send message after message asking about entrepreneurship, leadership, mindset: essentially every single other topic under the sun *except* for the one that I had just shared with you on stage! (*Marketing? We want to talk manifestation!* #Noted.)

Thank you for challenging me to go deeper beyond my composed "marketing expert" persona and wade into these scary, arctic waters of vulnerable stories and tough truths. I pray that the chapters of this book, structured using the questions you've bravely sent over the years, are exactly what you've been looking for. Because as Emma Thompson says, "Books are like people—they show up in your life when you need them the most." That has been 100 percent the case for me in my life, and it's my hope that the same is true for you. Thank you for allowing me to be the diametric opposite of perfect on the internet with you. Thank you for always showing up and sharing my *Highlights* podcasts, my Muse-letters, and my Lives and for trusting me with your most precious resource. Thank you for participating in our endless loop of digital love. Every message of triumph, of breakthrough, of joy, of reinvention, and especially of *recommitment* is truly #MyWhy.

A massive thank you to my agent, Jill. Your refusal to let me just phone anything in, skip a detail, or just say something was "good enough" (no matter how hard I tried to sell you on all of those) pushed this book to a level that would not have been possible without your vigilance. Thank you for never making me feel like my inexperience with the traditional publishing world was embarrassing or stupid. Thanks for letting me rant and rave ideas over the phone to you. Thanks for shooting down most of them. Thanks for identifying and unearthing the worthy nuggets buried deep (deep!) in our dialogue. Thanks for holding my hand through this whole process and being so patient. Saint Jill levels of kindness were exhibited, and I'm so grateful. Most of all, thank you for believing that this book possessed stories that needed to be shared with women around the world.

A massive thank you to my publishing team at McGraw Hill. Donya and Johnathan, you were fantastic to work with; thanks for guiding me through the process until Cheryl could rejoin us. Cheryl, your energy on this project was a godsend—thank you so much for taking the extra time to polish it for a Big Deal finish. I'm honored to be the recipient of your freshly rested momma brain and at the receiving end of your incredible energy to not settle for anything short of epic. You and your team totally rock.

To my friends and fam who suffered through 90 million rounds of feedback requests on everything from covers to titles to chapters—I can never repay you, but *thank you* for being so generous with your time and creative opinions. Mom, Seg, Bri-man, Lodg, Thelma, Mer, MKF, Aunt MB, Charlotte, Magpie, Sargie, Kimmers, Molly Murphy, Mike Ganino, Brian Fanzo, Jen Gitomer,

Judi Holler, LGO—your opinions and thoughts were *invaluable*. There is no way on God's green earth I could have ever made these big scary decisions without you retweeting or deleting every step of the way. Thank you for not blocking my phone number or Instagram. Yet.

To the first audacious woman I ever encountered: my mother. Mom, thank you for letting me ramble on and on about this book without taking a breath for months on end. Thanks for being brave enough to let me include our story in this book, even though you deeply value your privacy, and even though being "featured" in this way is legitimately your nightmare. I will never forget you sharing that Carly Simon moment back in the seventies sitting in your Chevette where she sang, "That's the way I always heard it should be." Recalling that flashback, you told me: "This is a message women needed to hear then, and they still need to hear it—now more than ever." That was a transcendent moment of unity and connection. That minute in time, with us working together as a team united by a shared mission, is seared lovingly into my brain for all time. I'm not sure whether or not you dug out your dog-eared nineties copy of *Parenting Your Strong-Willed Child* to sustain your sanity during the writing of this book, but if you did, I wouldn't fault you in the least. Thanks for the endless vocab flashcards, thanks for encouraging my love of reading (even into the wee hours of the night), and thanks for always telling me that as long as I spoke the truth—that you would always have my back. You again stood by that promise with your unconditional love and support during this project. I admire your fierce loyalty to our family and your unapologetic refusal to settle for anything subpar. You are the original Big

Deal woman. One thing we will always have in common is our unbreakable love for each other: because our relationship is forever worth fighting for. I love you, Momma.

To formerly known as Babygirl Seg: thank you for sharing your level-headed Libran diplomacy in helping me mold the stories of this book so they would not only ring true but also preserve peace and harmony within our ranks! Your honest, on-demand feedback these last few years was absolutely *vital* to this finished product. Thanks for actually reading all the massive multiscroll text messages and letting me word-vomit to you while I untangled the necklace of nuts that is often my mind. Your creativity, honesty, and generosity of time really meant the world to me. Your superpower of making everyone feel seen and not judged is truly a gift. I love you so much and can't believe I won the lady lottery of life to have you for my sister.

To the other ladies of the Trifecta. Sheena and Meredith—God must have been out of his mind the day He decided to bring the three of us together forever. No matter distances or life changes, the moments and milestones we have shared are the highlights of my life. The amount of wine, love, and laughter we've shared has to be illegal. At least in the country of Italy. Or in the state of Wyoming. Pretty much every story of my life (particularly the stories shared in this book) either begins or ends with our Trifecta. (Or at least has been analyzed, dissected, rehashed, and rewritten until the narrative is more to our liking.) My soul sister skates are still down in the garage. Let's just pray we have no need for them (or the dreaded onesies) for at least another 50 years.

To Sargie. Your love, support, and, most of all, spreadsheets have been the lifesaver of launching this book. Ever since our

Baltimore TV station days, I've admired your tenacity, your honesty, your hustle, and, of course, your incomparable heart. After almost 20 years of friendship, I can honestly say there's no one I'd rather put my toe on in the middle of the night than you. Not even Hartman. Thanks for being a champion of the mission behind this book, for allowing me to share your inspiring story, and for teaching me your winning ways. I adore you!

To Kimmy. You believed in me and helped me get this business off the ground at the most absolutely make-or-break pivotal point. Whether we are working together or not, are living in close proximity or not, have talked recently or not, we are always connected and you are always my heart. So far you have a 100 percent show-up rate in my books because you are the one when I first stumbled into the "real" world that I learned everything from. (And still do!) Thank you for letting me channel your superpowers for years until I discovered my own. Also, we need some new stories as Todd and Hartman are completely over the Amos collection. Hopefully, my readers feel differently. Love you, Kimmer.

To my SheNoters: Neen, Tamsen, and Tami—*thank you* for allowing me open access to your brilliant, award-winning brains. But beyond your generosity and creative wisdom, thank you for supporting me emotionally through this process and always dropping everything to work on a story or an idea, no matter how much you had going on with your own books, coaching, keynotes, families, and all. You were each just a text away reminding me that I was smart, capable, and good enough to actually make this thing. Thank you for inspiring me beyond words. I'm still not exactly sure how I got invited into a crew of this caliber, but fingers crossed I can keep fooling you all a little longer because we really do have all the fun.

Finally, the biggest Grand Teton–sized mountain of gratitude goes to my Harpi. Ever since that day on the beach when you told me I wasn't a particularly good manager, you rolled the dice of me dumping you on the spot to help me reveal what I was actually meant to do with my life. Thank you for never being scared of disappointing me with the truth. You showed me that I could lead from my experiences without investing so much time in spaces that stole my joy, spaces that were someone else's definition of success, and, most of all, spaces that were dumping my strengths down the drain instead of harnessing them. You helped me stop judging myself for my innumerable weaknesses and stay laser-focused on the light. You've always believed in me and my mission *way* before I ever even knew what it was. Thank you for always challenging me to "*Google it*" instead of allowing a single one of my BS excuses to take up an ounce of precious mental real estate. You constantly exemplify what it means to live as a true "student of life." Thank you for picking me up every single time I fall. Like, literally. Like the time you actually saved my life in the backcountry of Wyoming, and that other time with the fainting in France, and that other time with the panic attack, and . . . and . . . you are my actual, real-life superhero. Thank you for listening to me talk (*endlessly*) about this book, even though you would rather be programming AI computer vision machine-learning robots. (Did I get that right?) Thank you for doing anything and everything to build this business with me, one video editing session and DJ Ocean dance party at a time. You are my rock. You are my whole heart. I love you so deeply.

Thank you for being my forever Renaissance man. You are the Biggest Deal of them all.

(Wait, actually, that's not technically true. There's just *one* Bigger Deal than you.)

Thank you, God, for all your blessings and protection, and for the guidance of your angels that I feel every day. With You all things are possible.

READY FOR
THE BIG LEAGUES?

You know when you read a book and you're all fired up to make a big change in your life, and for the first few days (hours?) you *do*? But then pretty quickly life happens, and instead of feeling like kind of a Big Deal, you're kind of back in your old routine. Well, not this time, friend.

Like a new workout routine or a new healthy eating program, having an accountability partner is a powerful practice to achieving *actual* transformation. If only you had such a partner—someone who would lock arms with you and support you unlocking your BDE to truly revamp your everyday, someone who had a program designed to take the ideas from this book off the pages and into your life—*waving arms frantically*.

Welcome to the Big Leagues.

The Big Leagues is a 10-week coaching program designed to activate your audacity to overcome and level up in some of the most challenging areas of your life. Leadership, entrepreneurship, sales, marketing, relationships, communication, wellness—we cover it all. The 10 weeks are based on revisiting the key strategies from each chapter in this book, so you can extrapolate the lessons that spoke to you the most and put them into actual practice in real life.

Joining the Big Leagues is like hiring a team of accountability coaches to drive lasting progress in your personal and professional life. The Big Leagues experience involves daily text message motivation, weekly accountability challenges, and exclusive access to our Big League community. Our members consist of vetted, top-level entrepreneurs, network marketers, and small business owners who are firmly rocking the Team Abundance jersey. (This is the community where Team Scarcity mindsets go to die.)

Each week, I host a different, globally recognized Big Deal expert to help us tackle a new topic from a fresh perspective with a live, interactive Q&A experience. Big Deal Lives are limited live streams that include lessons, stories, challenges, affirmations, and so much more. Big Deal Lives are only available within our private community and are *not* available anywhere else on social media or online. Replays will be available for an on-demand boost, whether you are looking to maximize your day or motivate your team.

Learn more at bigleagues.erinking.com. (Exclusive reader code: BIGDEALBOOK.)

BIG DEAL BOOK CLUB

Dear book club hostess, thank you for selecting this book for your book club! As the classic saying goes: *There's a special place in heaven for women who help other women unlock their Big Deal Energy!* I can't wait for you to share all the #BigDealBook stories, insights, and impactful moments that stem from your special time together. Here's a few starter log questions to help you ignite the dialogue:

1. When do you naturally feel *most* like your Big Deal self in your life currently? Why?

2. When do you feel *least* like a Big Deal? Why do you think that is?

3. What is your biggest "superpower"?

4. What superpower do you wish you had more of in your life? Who do you know in your life that seems exceptionally superpowered in that area? Is there anything that person does that you could borrow or channel the next time you need it?

5. What is something that you feel afraid of on a daily basis or fairly regularly? (That is, not fear of death, but fear of not being seen by your siblings as successful enough, fear of being rejected by bosses or clients, fear of putting yourself out there again, etc.) Also beware that fear

sometimes shows up as worry, so pay attention to when you find yourself saying, "I just worry that . . ." Is your fear (or worry) rooted in a "feeling" or a "fact"?

6. Is there an area of your life where you feel drained beyond belief but you feel like you don't have a choice, because it's just something you "have" to do? What is it? Could you experiment with delegating that responsibility or lessening your role with it? Even if for just one time to see what would happen?

7. Is there something in your life that you have always dreamed of doing but for adulting purposes you just "can't"? Maybe it's an opportunity you regret not taking advantage of, a secret passion, or a wild fantasy, or maybe it's just asking for more damn money for a job or project? Why "can't" you? What would happen if you did it anyway? Which is worse: Is it the reaction or result that you've been trying to avoid, or Is it the nagging feeling that you never did chase down that desire?

8. When was the last time you got negative feedback? Was it maybe when you made a tough decision, started something new, or took a chance on something out of your comfort zone? Did that feedback have more to do with *you* or how your actions made that person feel? If that feedback was in response to something important to you or something you feel fairly clear about, how might you prepare yourself to ignore that feedback the next time?

9. What is your biggest goal or dream for the next 12 months of your life? What is one tangible thing you can purchase, start, complete, or *do* to signal to God (or the universe, the world, whatever you believe in) that your Big Deal self *is* manifesting this dream into existence?

10. When was the last time you felt jealous of someone? Was it a "healthy competition" jealousy or an "unhealthy comparison" one? If the latter, what is one thing you can do, think, or change to evolve it into the healthier, inspired version?

11. Who are the 5 to 10 people you are spending the most time with these days? If you had to assign them a jersey for Team Abundance (helping you) or Team Scarcity (hindering you), how many players would you have on each team in this game of your life? If you're handing out too many Scarcity jerseys, what is one step you can take to recruit a new member into your orbit for Team Abundance? (Obviously this could be a slightly awkward question depending on who is physically present at your book club. If so, you can assign this as follow up individual homework after your event.)

12. When was the last time you were working toward a goal with incredible focus? Did you ever feel lonely or like you were letting someone else down as an indirect result? Is there one thing you can do to make peace with that?

13. Please go back to question 7. What was your initial answer about what you really want to do, but you feel stuck or scared or you just "can't"?

14. What is one Big Deal action you could take to make your Big Deal dream come true? Is it a new routine, a new discipline, a mindset shift, a new behavior or habit? Maybe you need to leave something or somewhere or someone behind that is blocking your BDE? What, where, and who might that be?

See, here's the thing. Your entire book club and I know you possess the audacity within you to do this thing once and for all. We already know you're kind of a Big Deal. What we don't yet know is whether or not *you believe* that you are. And the minute you do, when you tap into your BDE to activate your audacity, *that* is the moment you unlock everything you've ever wanted. So say it with us, out loud, as many times as you need to until you believe it.

"*I'm kind of a Big Deal.*"

Yes, you are.

ADDITIONAL RESOURCES

Highlights with Erin King podcast

Leaders truly are readers *and yet* . . . not all leaders have the bandwidth to physically read an entire book. Particularly the bigger your leadership role becomes! This truth was the exact reason why I created a kind of "Cliff Notes for grownups" to showcase the biggest, juiciest ideas from the most transformative nonfiction books I've ever read. *Highlights with Erin King* is packed with the biggest takeaways right from the authors themselves. Glean the most impactful ideas in less than the time it takes to watch a show on Netflix. You can find the latest episodes of *Highlights with Erin King* on iTunes, Spotify, Stitcher, and Pandora.

Big Deal Swag

For those days where you need a little jump-start to your swagger, fire up your team with Big Deal Diaries, BDE mugs, BDE cozy yoga tops, everyday affirmation cards, and so much more. Gift some swag by checking out bigdeal.erinking.com.

Network Marketing/Leadership Trainings

Check out bigdealoffer.erinking.com to learn more about my Big Deal Training Trade. The idea is simple: order copies of #BigDealBook and unlock access to free sales, social media, and/or mindset trainings (plus swagger, course passes, events, and more). These "train the trainer" programs are ideal for learning how to teach my methods at scale with a repeatable, proven yet *creative* process.

Convention Keynotes

From intimate leadership retreats of a few hundred to pulsing convention center arenas of 20,000—if you are looking for a keynote speaker to take your organization on a ride of laughing, crying, and learning—erinking.com/keynotes is your hub for all things keynote: descriptions, sample videos, virtual and live demo reels, client testimonials, press kit, and more.

The Social Media Spa

If you are looking to level up your social media sales strategy, join me for a day at the Social Media Spa—where we clarify, detox, and refresh your messaging for maximum impact to your results and revenue. Learn the social media secrets I've shared with the world's top network marketing and Fortune 100 brands and influencers. Go to erinking.com and click "course" and use special reader code BIGDEALBOOK50 for 50 percent off of your lifetime access pass.

Digital Persuasion: Sell Smarter in the Modern Marketplace

If you're looking to help your team type, text, or tweet more powerfully, persuasively, and influentially, this book teaches my award-winning PUB method, which has helped teams from the Oscars in Hollywood to the US Navy at the Pentagon level up. Get your copy at erinking.com. For bulk discounts, message teamerin@erinking.com. The corresponding keynote to this book is ideal for B2B and B2C sales, marketing, and leadership conferences, as well as network marketing conferences.

Join Me on Clubhouse @erinking!

My friend LGO and I host *Level Up Live* every weekday at 8 a.m. PST/11 a.m. EST. Jump-start your mornings with us (as well as special surprise guests who pop in often) as we talk all things mindset and motivation to take our personal and professional lives to the next level.

INDEX

ABOUT THE AUTHOR

Erin King is a bestselling author, three-time entrepreneur, and podcaster who has helped clients from the Academy Awards to the US Navy communicate more persuasively online using her trademark PUB method.

She is the Amazon bestselling author of *Digital Persuasion* and started her first two companies—Jump Digital Media and PMS.com—before the age of 30. She is the founder of Socialite Agency, a social media firm that was featured in *Forbes*. Socialite's clients include ABC/Disney, Mercedes-Benz Fashion Week, VISA, Siemens, Hitachi, Mutual of Omaha, Johnson & Johnson, and dozens of others. Her podcast, *Highlights with Erin King,* discusses big ideas from the best nonfiction authors in the world, and has been described as an "audio Cliff Notes for grownups."

Way, way back in the Dark Ages, Erin competed in the World Irish Dancing Championships, played NCAA Division 1 lacrosse, and was a Johnny G (90s Peloton) spin instructor. But these pursuits were a walk in the park compared to being a brand-new dog mom to a precocious Cavapoo named Betty White. Off duty, Erin is playing outside in either Laguna Beach or Jackson Hole with her wild Southern husband, Hartman, or spending time with her huge, crazy Irish family. You might also find her hiding from all of the above behind the covers of a nice, good book. Learn about Erin's keynotes, courses, coaching, and more at www.erinking.com.

≥ MY BIG DEAL NOTES ≤

MY BIG DEAL NOTES

⇒ MY BIG DEAL NOTES ⇐

MY BIG DEAL NOTES

MY BIG DEAL NOTES